Diabetic Air Fryer Cookbook 2022

Proven, Delicious and Easy Diabetes Air Fryer Recipes for Beginners to Prepare Amazing Low Fat and Low Sugar to Manage Type 1 and Type 2 Diabetes. 21 Meal Plan.

Author: Sarah Jones

Legal Notice:

Copyright 2022 by Sarah Jones - All rights reserved.

This document is geared towards providing exact and reliable information regarding the topic and issue covered. The publication is sold on the idea that the publisher is not required to render an accounting, officially permitted, or otherwise, qualified services. If advice is necessary, legal or professional, a practiced individual in the profession should be ordered. From a Declaration of Principles which was accepted and approved equally by a Committee of the American Bar Association and a Committee of Publishers and Associations.

Legal Notes:

In no way is it legal to reproduce, duplicate, or transmit any part of this document by either electronic means or in printed format. Recording of this publication is strictly prohibited and any storage of this document is not allowed unless with written permission from the publisher. All rights reserved. The information provided herein is stated to be truthful and consistent, in that any liability, in terms of inattention or otherwise, by any usage or abuse of any policies, processes, or directions contained within is the solitary and utter responsibility of the recipient reader. Under no circumstances will any legal responsibility or blame be held against the publisher for any reparation, damages, or monetary loss due to the information herein, either directly or indirectly. Respective authors own all copyrights not held by the publisher.

Disclaimer Notice:

The information herein is offered for informational purposes solely and is universal as so. The presentation of the information is without a contract or any type of guarantee assurance. Readers acknowledge that the author is not engaging in the rendering of legal, financial, medical or professional advice. Please consult a licensed professional before attempting any techniques outlined in this book.

By continuing with this book, readers agree that the author is under no circumstances responsible for any losses, indirect or direct, that are incurred as a result of the information presented in this document, including, but not limited to inaccuracies, omissions and errors. The trademarks that are used are without any consent, and the publication of the trademark is without permission or backing by the trademark owner. All trademarks and brands within this book are for clarifying purposes only and are the owned by the owners themselves, not affiliated with this document.

Table of Contents

Introduction 8
- How Does Air Frying Work? 8
- Tips For Cooking with An Air Fryer 9
- What Are The Health Benefits Of Air-Fried Foods? 9
- What Does Air-Fried Food Taste Like? 10

Breakfast 14
1. Air Fried Eggs 15
2. Spinach and Mushrooms Omelette 16
3. Fennel Frittata 17
4. Cinnamon and Cheese Pancake 18
5. Scallion Sandwich 19
6. Asparagus Omelette 20
7. Pumpkin Pie French Toast 21
8. Breakfast Cheese Bread Cups 22
9. Breakfast Cod Nuggets 23
10. Oriental Omelette 24
11. Crispy Breakfast Avocado Fries 25
12. Baked Mini Quiche 26
13. Avocado and Blueberry Muffins 27
14. Bacon and Cheese Rolls 28
15. Bagels 29
16. Easy Breakfast Potatoes 30
17. Three Meat Cheesy Omelette 31
18. Masala Omelette the Indian Way 32
19. Air Fried Shirred Eggs 33

20. Air Fried Sourdough Sandwiches 34

Snacks and Appetizers 35

21. Vegetable Rolls 36
22. Cheesy Chicken Omelette 37
23. Cheesy Chickpea and Zucchini Burgers 38
24. Zucchini Crisps 39
25. Ripe Plantains 40
26. Garlic Cauliflower Nuggets 41
27. Cheese and Onion Nuggets 42
28. Onion Rings 43
29. Eggplant Fries 44
30. Garlic Salmon Balls 45
31. Blueberry Buns 46
32. Parmesan French Fries 47
33. Green Bell Peppers with Cauliflower Stuffing 48
34. Spicy Sweet Potatoes 49
35. Red Cabbage and Mushroom Stickers 50
36. Parmesan Cauliflower 51
37. Corn Tortilla Chips 52
38. Cream Buns with Strawberries 53
39. Garlic Roasted Mushrooms 54
40. Onion Bites 55

Lunch 56

41. Lemon-Garlic Chicken 57
42. Herb-Marinated Chicken Thighs 58
43. Blackened Chicken Breast 59

44. Air Fryer Brown Rice Chicken Fried 60
45. Chicken Thighs Smothered Style 61
46. Zucchini Turkey Burgers 62
47. Air Fryer Hamburgers 63
48. Taco-Stuffed Peppers 64
49. Flavourful Meatballs 65
50. Beef with Mushrooms 66
51. Lemon Greek Beef and Vegetables 67
52. Paprika Pulled Pork 68
53. Air Fryer Pork Chop & Broccoli 69
54. Cheesy Pork Chops in Air Fryer 70
55. Pork Trinova Wrapped in Ham 71
56. Stuffed Cabbage and Pork Loin Rolls 72
57. Asian Sesame Cod 73
58. Sriracha Calamari 74
59. Shrimp Rolls in Air Fryer 75
60. Lime-Garlic Shrimp Kebabs 76
61. Fish Finger Sandwich 77

Dinner 78
62. Catfish with Green Beans, in Southern Style 79
63. Parmesan Garlic Crusted Salmon 80
64. Air Fried Cajun Salmon 81
65. Lime Baked Salmon 82
66. Cajun Salmon 83
67. Chicken Pie 84
68. Air Fryer Brown Rice Chicken Fried 85

69. Buttermilk Chicken in Air-Fryer 86
70. Chicken with Mixed Vegetables 87
71. Lemon Rosemary Chicken 88
72. Air Fried Steak with Asparagus 89
73. Air Fry Rib-Eye Steak 90
74. Beef and Ale Casserole 91
75. Meatloaf 92
76. Lamb Chops with Herb Butter 93
77. Jamaican Jerk Pork 94
78. 12-Minute Pork Loin 95
79. Spiced Pork Chops 96
80. Herbed Pork Ribs 97
81. Pork Ribs 98

Desserts 99

82. Cheesecake Bites 100
83. Coconut Pie 101
84. Crustless Cheesecake 102
85. Chocolate Cake 103
86. Chocolate Brownies 104
87. Spiced Apples 105
88. Chocolate Lava Cake 106
89. Pecan Pie Bread Pudding 107
90. Apple Crumble Jars 108
91. Amaretto Cheesecake 109
92. Chocolate Soufflé for Two 111
93. Blueberry Lemon Muffins 112

94. Cinnamon Fried Bananas 113
95. Bacon and Maple Muffins 114
96. Air Fryer Brownies 115
97. Coconut Pie 116
98. Cheesecake Bites..117
99. Tahini Oatmeal Chocolate Chunk Cookies 118
100. Raspberry Cookies in Air Fryer 119
101. Banana Muffins in Air Fryer 120

Introduction

Patients with diabetes are typically recommended to avoid fried foods. Usually, fried foods are breaded, which adds carbohydrates, unhealthy fats, and calories from all the oil associated with deep frying. Adding too much fat to your diet can lead to weight gain, which can worsen diabetes.

According to the American Heart Association (AHA), weight gain also increases your risk of heart disease, which is already elevated in people with diabetes. Patients are usually encouraged to bake or roast these foods rather than eat breaded and fried favourites such as shrimp, chicken nuggets, onion rings, or fried okra.

Due to the upturn of technology in the kitchen appliance industry, however, fried foods no longer require a ton of oil. With air frying you are given the opportunity to enjoy the same crispy, delicious foods without the added oil or calories. Air fryers circulate scorching hot air throughout a cooking chamber, much like with a deep fryer would achieve using oil.

How Does Air Frying Work?

Air fryers use swirling hot air to cook food faster and more evenly instead of hot oil. In order to achieve the same golden brown, crispy crust you get when frying in oil, the food is placed in a wire mesh basket or on a rack to allow hot air to circulate evenly around the food.

The air fryer is easy to use, cooks' food faster than baking, and is easy to clean. You can cook a variety of everyday foods, including vegetables, meat, fish, eggs, and more, in addition to your favourite fried foods.

Tips For Cooking with An Air Fryer

- Make sure food is uniformly sized for even cooking.
- Food should be spread evenly, and thinly in the air fryer basket. The finished product may taste less crisp if the food is crowded.
- You can get the same golden brown, crispy crust by coating the surface with a thin layer of oil. Apply oil evenly to the food using a cooking spray or an oil mister. Alternatively, place the food in a bag and lightly coat it with a small amount of oil.
- You can also reheat foods in an air fryer, especially if they have a crispy crust that you want to keep crisp.

What Are The Health Benefits Of Air-Fried Foods?

It is generally considered healthier to air fry than to fry in oil. The calorie intake is reduced by 70% to 80% and the fat content is a lot lower.

In addition to reducing some of the health risks associated with oil frying, this method might also reduce the cost of cooking. In the process of frying starchy foods like potatoes, acrylamide is created, which is known to increase cancer risk. According to one study, air frying reduces acrylamide levels in fried potatoes by 90%.

There are some things about air frying you may not like, however. A study found that air-frying fish increased the amount of a substance called cholesterol oxidation products (COPs). Cooking breaks down the cholesterol in meat and fish, forming COPs. These substances are associated with cancer, hardening of the arteries, coronary heart disease, and other diseases.

What Does Air-Fried Food Taste Like?

Do air-fried foods taste as good as classic fried food? That's a matter of taste.

During frying, food absorbs any oil used to cook it. Fried foods retain moisture on the inside while maintaining their crispy exterior. Additionally, frying makes foods appear rich, dark, and appetizing to the eye.

The crunch is still there with air frying, but it doesn't have the same look or feel as oil frying. An oil-fry versus an air-fry study found that both methods produced foods with a similar moisture and colour content, however the textures and tastes varied.

You should also pay attention to your cooking technique. If you overcrowd the small basket, your food may cook unevenly, leaving some crunchy spots and some soggy ones.

The study suggests that adding fresh parsley, chives, or a mixture of the two will reduce the COPs when you air fry fish. Air-fried foods' COPs are reduced by these herbs acting as antioxidants.

Furthermore, air frying seems to reduce omega-3 fatty acids in fish. By lowering blood pressure and raising "good" HDL cholesterol and protecting the heart, these "good fats" may help lower blood pressure.

So, if you like fried foods, and would like to figure out interesting recipes you can enjoy daily, here are a few amazing meals you can enjoy during the next 21 days.

Day	Breakfast	Lunch	Dinner	Dessert/Snack
1	Air Fried Eggs & Bagels	Stuffed Cabbage and Pork Loin Rolls	Meatloaf	Zucchini Chips
2	Scallion Sandwich	Lemon Garlic Chicken	Spiced Pork Chops	Garlic Cauliflower Nuggets
3	Fennel Frittata	Air Fryer Hamburgers	Cajun Salmon	Blueberry Buns
4	Breakfast Cheese Bread Cups	Cheesy Pork Chops in Air Fryer	Air Fried Steak with Asparagus	Cheesy Chickpea and Zucchini Burgers
5	Oriental Omelette	Zucchini Turkey Burger	Jamaican Jerk Pork	Ripe Plantain
6	Pumpkin Pie French Toast	Taco-Stuffed Peppers	Lamb Chops with Herb Butter	Cheesecake Bites
7	Crispy Breakfast Avocado Fries	Paprika Pulled Pork	Pork Ribs	Apple Crumble Jars
8	Pumpkin Pie French Toast	Lemon Garlic Chicken	Meatloaf	Zucchini Chips

9	Breakfast Cod Nuggets	Stuffed Cabbage and Pork Loin Rolls	Spiced Pork Chops	Ripe Plantain
10	Baked Mini Quiche	Cheesy Pork Chops in Air Fryer	Air Fried Steak with Asparagus	Cheesecake Bites
11	Air Fried Eggs & Bagels	Paprika Pulled Pork	Cajun Salmon	Blueberry Buns
12	Crispy Breakfast Avocado Fries	Taco-Stuffed Peppers	Jamaican Jerk Pork	Coconut Pie
13	Oriental Omelette	Air Fryer Hamburgers	Meatloaf	Garlic Cauliflower Nuggets
14	Scallion Sandwich	Zucchini Turkey Burger	Lamb Chops with Herb Butter	Cheesy Chickpea and Zucchini Burgers
15	Pumpkin Pie French Toast	Taco-Stuffed Peppers	Air Fried Steak with Asparagus	Spiced Apples
16	Easy Breakfast Potatoes	Stuffed Cabbage and Pork Loin Rolls	Spiced Pork Chops	Pecan Pie Bread Pudding
17	Fennel Frittata	Lemon Garlic Chicken	Pork Ribs	Air Fryer Brownies

18	Breakfast Cod Nuggets	Cheesy Pork Chops in Air Fryer	Jamaican Jerk Pork	Ripe Plantain
19	Three Meat Cheesy Omelette	Zucchini Turkey Burger	Cajun Salmon	Zucchini Chips
20	Air Fried Shrimp Eggs	Air Fryer Hamburgers	Spiced Pork Chops	Garlic Cauliflower Nuggets
21	Crispy Breakfast Avocado Fries	Stuffed Cabbage and Pork Loin Rolls	Meatloaf	Blueberry Buns

Breakfast

1. Air Fried Eggs

Servings| 4   Time| 30minutes
Nutritional Content (per serving):
Cal| 106   Fat| 3g   Protein| 10g   Carbs| 10g

Ingredients:
- 4 eggs
- 60g (16oz) baby spinach, rinsed
- 1 tbsp. extra-virgin olive oil
- 130g (4.5oz) cheddar cheese, reduced fat, shredded, divided
- Bacon, sliced
- Pinch salt
- Pinch pepper

Directions:
1. Preheat the Air Fryer to 350°F (180°C).
2. Warm oil in a pan over medium-high flame. Cook the spinach until wilted. Drain the excess liquid. Put the cooked spinach into four greased ramekins.
3. Add a slice of bacon to each ramekin, crack an egg, and put cheese on top. Season with salt and pepper.
4. Put the ramekins inside the cooking basket of the Air Fryer. Cook for 15 minutes.

2. Spinach and Mushrooms Omelette

Servings| 4   Time| 21 minutes
Nutritional Content (per serving):
Cal| 109   Fat| 1g   Protein| 6g   Carbs| 8g

Ingredients:
- 15g (0.5oz) spinach leaves
- 90g (3oz) mushrooms
- 3 green onions
- 1 cup (250 ml) water
- ½ tsp. turmeric
- ½ red bell pepper
- 2 tbsp. butter, low fat
- 110g (4 oz) almond flour
- ½ tsp. onion powder
- ½ tsp. garlic powder
- ½ tsp. fresh ground black pepper
- ¼ tsp. ground thyme
- 2 tbsp. extra-virgin olive oil
- 1 tsp. black salt
- Salsa, store-bought

Directions:
1. Preheat the Air Fryer to 300°F (150°C). Rinse spinach leaves over tap water. Set aside.
2. In a mixing bowl, combine green onions, onion powder, garlic powder, red bell pepper, mushrooms, turmeric, thyme, olive oil, salt, and pepper. Mix well.
3. In another bowl, combine water and flour to form a smooth paste.
4. In a pan, heat olive oil. Sauté peppers and mushrooms for 3 minutes. Tip in spinach and cook for 3 minutes. Set aside.
5. Put in the air fryer basket our omelette batter. Cook for 3 minutes before flipping. Place vegetables on top.
6. Season with salt. Serve with salsa on the side.

3. Fennel Frittata

Servings| 6   Time| 20 minutes
Nutritional Content (per serving):
Cal| 199   Fat| 11g   Protein| 8g   Carbs| 5g

Ingredients:
- 1 fennel bulb; shredded
- 6 eggs; whisked
- 2 tsp. cilantro; chopped.
- 1 tsp. sweet paprika
- Cooking spray
- A pinch of salt and black pepper

Directions:
1. Take a bowl and mix all the ingredients except the cooking spray and stir well.
2. Grease a baking pan with the cooking spray, pour the frittata mix and spread well.
3. Put the pan in the Air Fryer and cook at 370°F (190°C) for 15 minutes. Divide between plates and serve them for breakfast.

4. Cinnamon and Cheese Pancake

Servings| 4   Time| 23 minutes
Nutritional Content (per serving):
Cal|139   Fat|10g   Protein|23g   Carbs|5g

Ingredients:
- 2 eggs
- 450g (16oz) cream cheese, reduced fat
- ½ tsp. cinnamon
- 1 pack Stevia

Directions:
1. Preheat Air Fryer to 330°F (165°C).
2. Meanwhile, combine cream cheese, cinnamon, eggs, and stevia in a blender.
3. Pour ¼ of the mixture in the air fryer basket. Cook for 2 minutes on each side. Repeat the process with the rest of the mix. Serve.

5. Scallion Sandwich

Servings|1   Time| 20 minutes
Nutritional Content (per serving):
Cal|154   Fat|2g   Protein|9g   Carbs|9g

Ingredients:
- 2 slices wheat bread
- 2 tsp. butter, low fat
- 2 scallions, sliced thinly
- 1 tbsp. parmesan cheese, grated
- 130g (4oz) cheddar cheese, reduced fat, grated

Directions:
1. Preheat the Air fryer to 356°F (180°C).
2. Spread butter on a slice of bread. Place inside the cooking basket with the butter side facing down.
3. Place cheese and scallions on top. Spread the rest of the butter on the other slice of bread, put it on top of the sandwich, and sprinkle with parmesan cheese. Cook for 10 minutes.

6. Asparagus Omelette

Servings| 2   Time| 20 minutes
Nutritional Content (per serving):
Cal|230   Fat| g   Protein| g   Carbs| g

Ingredients:
- 3 eggs
- 5 steamed asparagus tips
- 2 tbsp. of warm milk
- 1 tbsp. parmesan cheese, grated
- Salt and pepper, to taste
- Non-stick cooking spray

Directions:
1. Mix in a large bowl, eggs, cheese, milk, salt, and pepper, then blend them.
2. Spray a baking pan with non-stick cooking spray.
3. Transfer the mixture into the pan and add the asparagus, then place the pan inside the baking basket.
4. Set the air fryer to 320°F (160°C) for 8 minutes. Serve warm.

7. Pumpkin Pie French Toast

Servings|4   Time| 30 minutes
Nutritional Content (per serving):
Cal| 212   Fat| 8g   Protein| 12g   Carbs| 7g

Ingredients:
- 2 large, beaten eggs
- 4 slices cinnamon swirl bread
- ¼ cup (62.5 ml) milk
- 40g (1oz) pumpkin puree
- ¼ tsp. pumpkin spices
- 55 g (2oz) butter

Directions:
1. In a large mixing bowl, mix pumpkin puree, milk, eggs, and pie spice. Whisk until the mixture is smooth. In the egg mixture, dip the bread on both sides.
2. Place the rack inside of the air fryer's cooking basket. Place 2 slices of bread onto the rack.
3. Set the temperature to 340°F (175°C) for 10 minutes. Serve pumpkin pie toast with butter.

8. Breakfast Cheese Bread Cups

Servings|2   Time| 25 minutes
Nutritional Content (per serving):
Cal|161   Fat| 8g   Protein| 12g   Carbs| 10g

Ingredients:
- 2 eggs
- 2 tbsp. cheddar cheese, grated
- Salt and pepper, to taste
- 1 ham slice, cut into 2 pieces
- 4 bread slices, flatten with a rolling pin

Directions:
1. Spray the inside of 2 ramekins with cooking spray.
2. Place 2 flat pieces of bread into each ramekin. Add the ham slice pieces into each ramekin.
3. Crack an egg in each ramekin, then sprinkle with cheese. Season with salt and pepper.
4. Place the ramekins into the air fryer at 300°F (150°C) for 15 minutes. Serve warm.

9. Breakfast Cod Nuggets

Servings|4   Time| 20 minutes
Nutritional Content (per serving):
Cal| 213   Fat| 12g   Protein| 14g   Carbs| 9

Ingredients:
- 455g (16oz) cod

For breading:
- 2 eggs, beaten
- 2 tbsp. olive oil
- 125g (4oz) almond flour
- 80 g (3oz) breadcrumbs
- 1 tsp. dried parsley
- Pinch sea salt
- ½ tsp. black pepper

Directions:
1. Preheat the air fryer to 390°F (200°C).
2. Cut the cod into strips about 1-inch by 2-inches. Blend breadcrumbs, olive oil, salt, parsley, and pepper in a food processor.
3. In 3 separate bowls, add breadcrumbs, eggs, and flour. Place each piece of fish into flour, then the eggs, and the breadcrumbs.
4. Add pieces of cod to the air fryer basket and cook for 10 minutes. Serve warm.

10. Oriental Omelette

Servings|1   Time| 35 minutes
Nutritional Content (per serving):
Cal|210   Fat| 11g   Protein| 13g   Carbs| 8

Ingredients:
- 65g (2oz) fresh Shimeji mushrooms, sliced
- 2 eggs, whisked
- Salt and pepper, to taste
- 1 clove garlic, minced
- A handful of sliced tofu
- 2 tbsp. onion, finely chopped
- Cooking spray

Directions:
1. Spray the baking dish with cooking spray. Add onions and garlic. Air fry in the preheated air fryer at 355°F (180°C) for 4 minutes.
2. Place the tofu and mushrooms over the onions and add salt and pepper to taste.
3. Whisk the eggs and pour them over tofu and mushrooms. Air fry again for 20 minutes. Serve warm.

11. Crispy Breakfast Avocado Fries

Servings|2   Time| 16 minutes
Nutritional Content (per serving):
Cal|272   Fat| 13g   Protein| 16g   Carbs| 11g

Ingredients:
- 2 eggs, beaten
- 2 large avocados, peeled, pitted, cut into 8 slices each
- ¼ tsp. pepper
- ½ tsp. cayenne pepper
- Salt, to taste
- ½ a lemon, Juice
- 55g (2oz) whole-wheat flour
- 105g (4oz) whole-wheat breadcrumbs
- Greek yogurt to serve

Directions:
1. Add flour, salt, pepper, and cayenne pepper to bowl and mix. Add breadcrumbs into another bowl. Beat eggs in a third bowl.
2. First, dredge the avocado slices in the flour mixture. Next, dip them into the egg mixture, and finally dredge them in the breadcrumbs.
3. Place avocado fries into the air fryer basket. Preheat the air fryer to 390°F (200°C).
4. Place the air fryer basket into the air fryer and cook for 6 minutes.
5. When Cooking Time is completed, transfer the avocado fries onto a serving platter.
6. Sprinkle with lemon juice and serve with Greek yogurt.

12. Baked Mini Quiche

Servings|2   Time| 25 minutes
Nutritional Content (per serving):
Cal| 261   Fat| 8g   Protein| 10g   Carbs| 7g

Ingredients:
- 2 eggs
- 1 large yellow onion, diced
- 200g (7oz) whole-wheat flour
- 255g (9oz) spinach, chopped
- 190g (7oz) cottage cheese
- Salt and black pepper, to taste
- 2 tbsp. olive oil
- 160g (6oz) butter
- 185g (6oz) milk

Directions:
1. Preheat the air fryer to 355°F (180°C). Add the flour, butter, salt, and milk to the bowl and knead the dough until smooth and refrigerate for 15 minutes.
2. Abode a frying pan over medium heat and add the oil to it.
3. When the oil is heated, add the onions into the pan and sauté them. Introduce spinach to the pan and cook until it wilts.
4. Drain the excess moisture from spinach. Whisk the eggs together and add cheese to the bowl, and mix.
5. Take the dough out of the fridge and divide it into eight equal parts. Roll the dough into a ball that will fit into the bottom of the quiche mound.
6. Place the rolled dough into moulds. Place the spinach filling over the dough.
7. Place moulds into air fryer basket and place basket inside of air fryer and cook for 15 minutes.
8. Remove quiche from moulds and serve warm or cold.

13. Avocado and Blueberry Muffins

Servings|12   Time| 20 minutes
Nutritional Content (per serving):
Cal|202   Fat| 9g   Protein| 6g   Carbs| 7g

Ingredients:
- 2 eggs
- 55g (2oz) blueberries
- 250g (9oz) almond flour
- 1 tsp. baking soda
- ⅛ tsp. salt
- 2 ripe avocados, peeled, pitted, mashed
- 2 tbsp. liquid Stevia
- 500g (18oz) plain Greek yogurt
- 1 tsp. vanilla extract

For the streusel topping:
- 2 tbsp. Truvia sweetener
- 4 tbsp. butter, softened
- 4 tbsp. almond flour

Directions:
1. Make the streusel topping by mixing Truvia, flour, and butter until you form a crumbly mixture. Place it in the freezer for a while.
2. Meanwhile, make the muffins by sifting together flour, baking powder, baking soda, and salt, and set aside. Add avocados and liquid Stevia to a bowl and mix well. Adding in one egg at a time, continue to beat. Add the vanilla extract and yogurt and beat again.
3. Add in flour mixture a bit at a time and mix well. Add the blueberries into the mixture and gently fold them in. Pour the batter into greased muffin cups, then add the mixture until they are half-full.
4. Sprinkle the streusel topping mixture on top of the muffin mixture and place muffin cups in the air fryer basket.
5. Bake in the preheated air fryer at 355°F (180°C) for 10 minutes. Remove the muffin cups from the air fryer and allow them to cool. Cool completely, then serve.

14. Bacon and Cheese Rolls

Servings|4   Time| 20 minutes
Nutritional Content (per serving):
Cal|231   Fat| 7g   Protein| 13   Carbs| 6

Ingredients:
- 455g (1 lb.) cheddar cheese, grated
- 455g (1 lb.) bacon rashers
- 1 can (8 oz.) Pillsbury Crescent dough

Directions:
1. Warm up the Air Fryer to 330°F (165°C).
2. Cut the bacon rashers across into ¼ inch strips and mix with the cheddar cheese. Set aside.
3. Cut the dough sheet to 1 by 1.5 inches pieces. Place an equal amount of bacon and cheese mixture on the centre of the dough pieces and pinch corners together to enclose stuffing.
4. Transfer the parcels in the Air Fry basket and bake for 7 minutes at 330°F (165°C).
5. Increase the temperature to 390°F (200°C) and bake for another 3 minutes. Serve warm.

15. Bagels

Servings|12   Time| 40 minutes
Nutritional Content (per serving):
Cal| 232   Fat| 8g   Protein| 13g   Carbs| 6g

Ingredients:
- 230g (½ lb.) flour
- 1 tsp. active dry yeast
- 1 tsp. brown sugar
- ½ cup (125ml) lukewarm water
- 2 tbsp. butter softened
- 1 tsp. salt
- 1 large egg

Directions:
1. Liquefy the yeast and sugar in the warm water. Let rest for 5 minutes.
2. Add the remaining ingredients and mix until sticky dough forms. Cover and let rest for 40 minutes.
3. Massage the dough on a lightly floured surface and divide it into 5 large balls. Let rest for 4 minutes.
4. Preheat air fryer to 360°F (185°C).
5. Flatted the dough balls and make a hole in the centre of each. Arrange the bagels on a baking sheet lined with parchment paper. Bake for 20 minutes.

16. Easy Breakfast Potatoes

Servings|6   Time| 45 minutes
Nutritional Content (per serving):
Cal| 128   Fat| 0g   Protein| 3g   Carbs| 30 g

Ingredients:
- 4 large potatoes, cubed
- 2 bell peppers, cut into 1-inch chunks
- ½ onion, diced
- 2 tsp olive oil, 1 garlic clove Minced
- ½ tsp dried thyme
- ½ tsp cayenne pepper Salt to taste.

Directions:
1. Preheat the air fryer to 390°F (200°C). Place the potato cubes in a bowl and sprinkle with garlic, cayenne pepper, and salt.
2. Drizzle with some olive oil and toss to coat. Arrange the potatoes in an even layer in the greased frying basket.
3. Air Fry for 10 minutes, shaking once halfway through cooking.
4. In the meantime, add the remaining olive oil, garlic, thyme, and salt in a mixing bowl. Add in the bell peppers and onion and mix well.
5. Pour the veggies over the potatoes and continue cooking for 10 more minutes.
6. At the 5-minute mark, shake the basket and cook for 5 minutes. Serve warm.

17. Three Meat Cheesy Omelette

Servings|2   Time| 20 minutes
Nutritional Content (per serving):
Cal| 1210   Fat| 94g   Protein| 70g   Carbs| 21g

Ingredients:
- 1 beef sausage, chopped
- 4 slices prosciutto, chopped
- 85g (3oz) salami, chopped
- 260g (9oz) mozzarella cheese, grated
- 4 eggs
- 1 green onion, chopped
- 1 tbsp. ketchup
- 1 tsp. fresh parsley, chopped

Directions:
1. Preheat the air fryer to 350°F (180°C). Whisk the eggs with ketchup in a bowl. Stir in the green onion, mozzarella, salami, and prosciutto.
2. Air Fry the sausage in a greased baking pan inside the fryer for 2 minutes. Slide out and pour the egg mixture over.
3. Bake for 8-10 more minutes until golden. Serve topped with parsley.

18. Masala Omelette the Indian Way

Servings| 1   Time| 30 minutes
Nutritional Content (per serving):
Cal| 230   Fat| 15g   Protein| 14g   Carbs| 10g

Ingredients:
- 1 garlic clove, crushed
- 1 green onion
- ½ chili powder
- ½ tsp. garam masala
- 2 eggs
- 1 tbsp. olive oil
- 1 tbsp. fresh cilantro, chopped
- salt and black pepper to taste

Directions:
1. Preheat the air fryer to 360°F (185°C). In a bowl, whisk the eggs with salt and black pepper.
2. Add in the green onion, garlic, chili powder, and garam masala; stir well. Transfer to a greased baking pan.
3. Bake in the fryer for 8 minutes until the top is golden and the eggs are set. Scatter with fresh cilantro and serve

19. Air Fried Shirred Eggs

Servings| 2 Time| 30 minutes
Nutritional Content (per serving):
Cal| 177   Fat| 10g   Protein| 12g   Carbs| 11g

Ingredients:
- 2 tsp. butter, melted
- 4 eggs
- 2 tbsp. heavy cream
- 4 smoked ham slices
- 3 tbsp. Parmesan cheese, grated
- ¼ tsp. paprika
- Salt and black pepper to taste
- 2 tsp. fresh chives, chopped

Directions:
1. Preheat the air fryer to 320°F (160°C). Lightly grease 4 ramekins with butter.
2. Line the bottom of each ramekin with a piece of smoked ham.
3. Crack the eggs on top of the ham and season with salt and pepper. Drizzle with heavy cream and sprinkle with Parmesan cheese.
4. Air Fry for 10-12 minutes until the eggs are completely set.
5. Garnish with paprika and fresh chives to serve.

20. Air Fried Sourdough Sandwiches

Servings| 2   Time| 30 minutes
Nutritional Content (per serving):
Cal| 210   Fat| 8g   Protein| 9g   Carbs| 25g

Ingredients:
- 4 slices sourdough bread
- 2 tbsp. mayonnaise
- 2 slices ham
- 2 lettuce leaves
- 1 tomato, sliced
- 2 slices mozzarella cheese

Directions:
1. Preheat the air fryer to 350°F (180°C). On a clean working board, lay the bread slices and spread them with mayonnaise.
2. Top 2 of the slices with ham, lettuce leaves, tomato slices, and mozzarella. Cover with the remaining bread slices to form two sandwiches.
3. Air Fry for 12 minutes, flipping once. Serve hot.

Snacks and Appetizers

21. Vegetable Rolls

Servings| 4   Time| 20 minutes
Nutritional Content (per serving):
Cal| 125   Fat| 15g   Protein| 12g   Carbs| 8g

Ingredients:
- Toasted sesame seeds
- 2 carrots, grated
- Spring roll wrappers
- One egg white
- A dash gluten-free soy sauce
- Half cabbage, sliced
- 2 tbsp. Olive oil

Directions:
1. In a pan over high flame heat, 2 tbsp. of oil and sauté the chopped vegetables. Add soy sauce, turn off the heat, and add toasted sesame seeds.
2. Lay rolls on a surface and spread egg white with a brush. Add some vegetable mix in the wrapper and fold.
3. Spray the rolls with oil spray and cook in the Air Fryer for 8 minutes at 380°F (195°C).

22. Cheesy Chicken Omelette

Servings| 2   Time| 25 minutes
Nutritional Content (per serving):
Cal| 185   Fat| 150g   Protein| 20g   Carbs| 9g

Ingredients:

- 65g (2oz) Cooked Chicken Breast, diced
- Four eggs
- 1/4 tsp. Onion powder
- 1/2 tsp. Salt
- 1/4 tsp. Pepper
- 2 tbsp. Shredded cheese
- 1/4 tsp. Garlic powder

Directions:
1. Take two ramekins, grease with olive oil. Divided all ingredients in 2 portions.
2. Add two eggs to each ramekin. Add cheese, onion powder, salt, pepper, garlic and blend to combine. Add 1/4 cup of cooked chicken on top.
3. Cook at 330°F (165°C) for 14-18 minutes in the air fryer.

23. Cheesy Chickpea and Zucchini Burgers

Servings| 4   Time| 22 minutes
Nutritional Content (per serving):
Cal| 184   Fat| 10g   Protein| 13g   Carbs| 18g

Ingredients:

- 1 can chickpeas, drained
- 3 tbsp. coriander
- 30g (1oz.) cheddar cheese, shredded
- 2 eggs, beaten
- 1 tsp. garlic puree
- 1 zucchini spiralized
- 1 red onion, diced
- 1 tsp. chili powder
- 1 tsp. mixed spice
- Salt and pepper to taste
- 1 tsp. cumin

Directions:
1. Mix all the ingredients in a mixing bowl.
2. Shape portions of the mixture into burgers. Place in the air fryer at 300ºF (150°C) for 15 minutes.

24. Zucchini Crisps

Servings| 2   Time| 60 minutes
Nutritional Content (per serving):
Cal| 15   Fat| 0g   Protein| 1g   Carbs| 3g

Ingredients:
- 2 zucchinis, sliced into a ⅛-inch thick disk
- Pinch sea salt
- White pepper to taste
- 1 tbsp. of olive oil for drizzling

Directions:
1. Preheat the air fryer to 330°F (165°C).
2. Place zucchini in a bowl with salt. Let them drain in a colander for 30 minutes.
3. Layer zucchini in an overproof dish. Drizzle with oil and season with pepper. Place baking dish in the air fryer basket and cook for 30 minutes.
4. Adjust seasoning and serve.

25. Ripe Plantains

Servings| 2   Time| 20 minutes
Nutritional Content (per serving):
Cal| 209   Fat| 8g   Protein| 4g   Carbs| 29g

Ingredients:
- 2 pcs. ripe plantain, peeled and sliced
- 1 tbsp. coconut butter, unsweetened

Directions:
1. Preheat the air fryer to 350°F (180°C). Brush a small amount of coconut butter on all sides of plantain disks.
2. Place one even layer into the air fryer basket, making sure none overlap or touch. Fry plantains for 10 minutes.
3. Remove from the basket. Place on plates. Repeat steps for all plantains. While plantains are still warm. Serve.

26. Garlic Cauliflower Nuggets

Servings| 4   Time| 30 minutes
Nutritional Content (per serving):
Cal| 18   Fat| 1g   Protein| 2g   Carbs| 1g

Ingredients:
- 1 crown cauliflower, chopped in a food processor
- 130g (5oz) parmesan cheese, grated
- Salt and pepper to taste
- 50g (2oz) almond flour
- 2 eggs
- 1 tsp. garlic, minced

Directions:
1. Mix all the ingredients. Shape into nuggets and spray with olive oil. Preheat your air fryer to 400ºF (205°C).
2. Cook for 10 minutes on each side.

27. Cheese and Onion Nuggets

Servings| 4   Time| 20 minutes
Nutritional Content (per serving):
Cal| 226   Fat| 17g   Protein| 14g   Carbs| 4g

Ingredients:
- 200g (7oz.) Edam cheese, grated
- 2 spring onions, diced
- 1 egg, beaten
- 1 tbsp. coconut oil
- 1 tbsp. thyme, dried
- Salt and pepper to taste

Directions:
1. Mix the oil, cheese, thyme, onion, salt, and pepper in a bowl. Make 8 balls and place the Edam cheese in the centre.
2. Place in the fridge for an hour. With a pastry brush, brush the beaten egg over the nuggets. Cook for 12 minutes in the air fryer at 350ºF (180C).

28. Onion Rings

Servings| 3   Time| 20 minutes
Nutritional Content (per serving):
Cal| 303   Fat| 18g   Protein| 37g   Carbs| 32g

Ingredients:
- 1 onion, cut into slices, separate into rings
- 245g (9oz) milk
- 180g (6oz) pork rinds
- 120g (4oz) almond flour
- 1 egg
- 1 tbsp. baking powder
- ½ tsp. salt

Directions:
1. Preheat your air fryer for 10 minutes. Slice onion, then separate into rings. In a bowl, integrate the baking powder, flour, and salt.
2. Beat in the eggs and milk, then combines with the flour. Dip the onion rings into the batter to coat them.
3. Spread the pork rinds on a plate and dip the rings into the crumbs. Place the onion rings in your air fryer and cook for 10 minutes at 360ºF (185°C).

29. Eggplant Fries

Servings| 3   Time| 20 minutes
Nutritional Content (per serving):
Cal| 102   Fat| 7g   Protein| 2g   Carbs| 11g

Ingredients:
- 2 eggplants
- 55g (2oz) olive oil
- 24g (1oz) almond flour
- 40g (1oz) wate

Directions:
1. Preheat your air fryer to 390ºF (200°C). Cut the eggplants into ½-inch slices. In a mixing bowl, mix the water, flour, olive oil, and eggplants.
2. Coat the eggplants and add them to the air fryer and cook for 12 minutes. Serve with yogurt or tomato sauce.

30. Garlic Salmon Balls

Servings| 2   Time| 20 minutes
Nutritional Content (per serving):
Cal| 218   Fat| 8g   Protein| 22g   Carbs| 14g

Ingredients:
- 170g (6oz.) tinned salmon
- 1 large egg
- 3 tbsp. olive oil
- 5 tbsp. wheat germ
- ½ tsp. garlic powder
- 1 tbsp. dill, fresh, chopped
- 4 tbsp. spring onion, diced
- 4 tbsp. celery, diced

Directions:
1. Preheat your air fryer to 370ºF (190°C). In a large bowl, mix the salmon, egg, celery, onion, dill, and garlic.
2. Shape the mixture into small balls and roll in the wheat germ. In a small skillet, warm olive oil over medium-low heat.
3. Add the salmon balls and slowly flatten them. Handover them to your air fryer and cook for 10 minutes.

31. Blueberry Buns

Servings| 6   Time| 22 minutes
Nutritional Content (per serving):
Cal| 104   Fat| 2g   Protein| 2g   Carbs| 19g

Ingredients:
- 240g (8oz) all-purpose flour
- 50g (2oz) granulated sugar
- 8g (0.3oz) baking powder
- 2½ g (0.07oz) salt
- 85g (3oz) chopped cold butter
- 85g (3oz) fresh blueberries
- 5g (0.1oz) grated fresh ginger
- ½ cup (125ml) whipping cream
- 2 large eggs
- 1 tsp vanilla extract
- 1 tsp water

Directions:
1. Put sugar, flour, baking powder and salt in a large bowl.
2. Put the butter with the flour using a blender or your hands until the mixture resembles thick crumbs.
3. Mix the blueberries and ginger in the flour mixture and set aside.
4. Mix the whipping cream, 1 egg and the vanilla extract in a different container.
5. Put the cream mixture with the flour mixture until combined.
6. Shape the dough until it reaches a thickness of approximately 38 mm and cut it into eighths.
7. Spread the buns with a combination of egg and water. Set aside Preheat the air fryer set it to 380°F (195°C).
8. Place baking paper in the preheated inner basket and place the buns on top of the paper. Cook for 12 minutes.

32. Parmesan French Fries

Servings| 16   Time| 25 minutes
Nutritional Content (per serving):
Cal| 209   Fat| 5g   Protein| 7g   Carbs| 35g

Ingredients:
- 2 russet potatoes, washed
- 1 tbsp. olive oil
- 1 tbsp. garlic, granulated
- 65g (2oz) Parmesan cheese, grated
- 1/4 tsp. salt
- 1/4 tsp. ground black pepper
- 1 tbsp. fresh parsley, finely chopped (optional)

Directions:
1. Cut the potatoes into thin wedges and place them in a bowl. Drizzle the oil over the russet potatoes and toss to coat.
2. Sprinkle with the garlic, Parmesan cheese, salt, and pepper, and toss again.
3. Place in the air fryer basket and cook at 400ºF (205°C) for 20 minutes, stirring halfway through to ensure even cooking.
4. Top with the parsley and serve warm.

33. Green Bell Peppers with Cauliflower Stuffing

Servings| 4   Time| 17 minutes
Nutritional Content (per serving):
Cal| 257   Fat| 4g   Protein| 13g   Carbs| 44g

Ingredients:

- 4 green bell peppers, top cut, deseeded
- 1 tsp. lemon juice
- 2 tbsp. coriander leaves, finely chopped
- 2 green chilies, finely chopped
- 515g (18oz) cauliflower, cooked and mashed
- 2 onions, finely chopped
- 1 tsp. cumin seeds
- 1/4 tsp. turmeric powder
- 1/4 tsp. chili powder
- 1/4 tsp. garam masala
- Salt to taste
- Olive oil as needed

Directions:

1. In a saucepan, warm the oil and sauté the chilies, onion, and cumin seeds. Swell the rest of the ingredients except the bell peppers and mix well.
2. Preheat the air fryer to 390ºF (200°C) for 10 minutes.
3. Brush the green bell peppers with olive oil inside and out and stuff each pepper with cauliflower mixture.
4. Place them into the air fryer and grill for 10 minutes.

34. Spicy Sweet Potatoes

Servings| 4   Time| 30 minutes
Nutritional Content (per serving):
Cal| 303   Fat| 5g   Protein| 9g   Carbs| 57g

Ingredients:
- 3 sweet potatoes, peeled and chopped into chips
- 1 tsp. chili powder
- 1 tsp. paprika
- 2 tbsp. olive oil
- 1 tbsp. red wine vinegar
- 1 tomato, thinly sliced
- 125g (4oz) tomato sauce
- 1 onion, peeled and diced
- Salt and pepper to taste
- 1 tsp. rosemary
- 1 tsp. oregano
- 1 tsp. mixed spice
- 2 tsp. thyme
- 2 tsp. coriander

Directions:
1. Toss the chips in a bowl with olive oil. Add to the air fryer and cook for 15 minutes at 360ºF (185°C).
2. Mix the remaining ingredients in a baking dish. Place the sauce in the air fryer for 8 minutes.
3. Toss the potatoes in the sauce and serve warm.

35. Red Cabbage and Mushroom Stickers

Servings| 12   Time| 30 minutes
Nutritional Content (per serving):
Cal| 88   Fat| 3g   Protein| 3g   Carbs| 14g

Ingredients:

- 180g (6oz) red cabbage, shredded
- 45g (2oz) button mushrooms, chopped
- 45g (2oz) carrot, grated
- 2 tbsp. onion, minced
- 2 garlic cloves, minced
- 2 tsp. fresh ginger, grated
- 12 Gyoza potsticker wrappers
- 2 1/2 tsp. olive oil, divided
- 1 tbsp. water

Directions:

1. Combine the red cabbage, mushrooms, carrot, onion, garlic, and ginger in a baking pan.
2. Add 1 tbsp. of water. Place in the air fryer and bake at 370ºF (190°C) for 6 minutes, until the vegetables are crisp-tender. Drain and set aside.
3. Working one at a time, place the potsticker wrappers on a work surface. Top each wrapper with a scant 1 tbsp. of the filling.
4. Fold half of the wrapper over the other half to form a half-circle. Dab with water and press both edges together.
5. Spread 1 1/4 tsp. of olive oil on the baking pan. Put half of the potstickers, seam-side up, in the pan. Air fry for 5 minutes. Add 1 tbsp. of water and return the pan to the air fryer.
6. Air fry for 4 minutes more, or until hot. Repeat with the remaining potstickers, the remaining 1 1/4 tsp. of oil, and another tbsp. of water. Serve immediately.

36. Parmesan Cauliflower

Servings| 20   Time| 22 minutes
Nutritional Content (per serving):
Cal| 106   Fat| 6g   Protein| 4g   Carbs| 10g

Ingredients:
- 680g (24oz) cauliflower florets
- 100g (4oz) whole-wheat breadcrumbs
- 1 tsp. coarse sea salt or kosher salt
- 65g (2oz) Parmesan cheese, grated
- 55g (2oz) butter
- 65g (2oz) mild hot sauce
- Olive oil spray

Directions:
1. Place a parchment liner in the air fryer basket. Cut the cauliflower florets in half and set them aside.
2. In a small bowl, mix the breadcrumbs, salt, and Parmesan; set aside.
3. In a small microwave-safe bowl, combine the hot sauce and butter. Heat in the microwave until the butter is melted, about 15 seconds. Whisk.
4. Holding the stems of the cauliflower florets, dip them in the butter mixture to coat. Shake off any excess mixture.
5. Dredge the dipped florets with the bread crumb mixture, then put them in the air fryer basket. There's no need for a single layer; just toss them all in there.
6. Spray the cauliflower lightly with olive oil and air fry at 350ºF (180°C) for 15 minutes, shaking the basket a few times throughout the cooking process.
7. The florets are done when they are lightly browned and crispy. Serve warm.

37. Corn Tortilla Chips

Servings| 4   Time| 13 minutes
Nutritional Content (per serving):
Cal| 72   Fat| 4g   Protein| 2g   Carbs| 8g

Ingredients:
- 4 (6-inch) corn tortillas
- 1 tbsp. canola oil
- 1/4 tsp. kosher salt

Directions:
1. Stack the corn tortillas, cut them in half, then slice them into thirds.
2. Spray the air fryer basket with non-stick cooking spray, brush the tortillas with canola oil and place them in the basket. Air fry at 360ºF (185°C) for 5 minutes.
3. Pause the fryer to shake the basket, then air fry for 3 more minutes or until golden brown and crispy.
4. Remove the chips from the fryer and place them on a plate lined with a paper towel. Sprinkle with the kosher salt on top before serving warm.

38. Cream Buns with Strawberries

Servings| 6   Time| 22 minutes
Nutritional Content (per serving):
Cal| 149   Fat| 13g   Protein| 11g   Carbs| 3g

Ingredients:
- 240g (8oz) all-purpose flour
- 50g (2oz) granulated sugar
- 8g (0.3oz) baking powder
- 1g (0.04oz) salt
- 85g (3oz) chopped cold butter
- 85g (3oz) chopped fresh strawberries
- ½ cup (125ml) whipping cream
- 2 large eggs
- 2 tsp. vanilla extract
- 1 tsp. water

Directions:
1. Sift flour, sugar, baking powder and salt in a large bowl. Put the butter with the flour with the use of a blender or your hands until the mixture resembles thick crumbs.
2. Mix the strawberries in the flour mixture. Set aside for the mixture to stand. Beat the whipping cream, 1 egg and the vanilla extract in a separate bowl.
3. Put the cream mixture in the flour mixture until they are homogeneous, and then spread the mixture to a thickness of 38 mm.
4. Use a round cookie cutter to cut the buns. Spread the buns with a combination of egg and water. Set aside
5. Preheat the air fryer, set it to 375°F (190°C).
6. Place baking paper in the preheated inner basket. Place the buns on top and cook for 12 minutes.

39. Garlic Roasted Mushrooms

Servings| 4   Time| 25 minutes
Nutritional Content (per serving):
Cal| 128   Fat| 4g   Protein| 14g   Carbs| 17g

Ingredients:
- 16 garlic cloves, peeled
- 2 tsp. olive oil, divided
- 16 button mushrooms
- 1/2 tsp. marjoram, dried
- 1/8 tsp. freshly ground black pepper
- 1 tbsp. white wine or low-sodium vegetable broth

Directions:
1. In a baking pan, mix the garlic with 1 tsp. of olive oil. Roast in the air fryer at 350°F (180°C) for 12 minutes.
2. Add the mushrooms, marjoram, and pepper; stir to coat.
3. Drizzle with the remaining 1 tsp. of olive oil and white wine. Return to the air fryer and roast for 10 minutes more, or until the mushrooms and garlic cloves are tender. Serve.

40. Onion Bites

Servings| 20   Time| 20 minutes
Nutritional Content (per serving):
Cal| 166   Fat| 2g   Protein| 6g   Carbs| 31g

Ingredients:
- 20 white boiler onions
- 1 cup (250ml) buttermilk
- 2 eggs
- 125g (4oz) flour
- 105g (4oz) whole-wheat breadcrumbs
- 1 tbsp. smoked paprika
- 1 tsp. salt
- 1 tsp. ground black pepper
- 1 tsp. garlic, granulated
- 3/4 tsp. chili powder
- Olive oil spray

Directions:
1. Place a parchment liner in the air fryer basket.
2. Slice off the root end of the onions, taking off as little as possible.
3. Peel off the papery skin and make cuts halfway through the tops of the onions. Don't cut too far down; you want the onion to hold together still. In a large bowl, beat the buttermilk and eggs together.
4. Mix the flour, breadcrumbs, paprika, salt, pepper, garlic, and chili powder in a medium bowl.
5. Add the prepared onions to the buttermilk mixture and allow to soak for at least 10 minutes.
6. Remove the onions from the batter and dredge them with the bread crumb mixture.
7. Place the prepared onions in the air fryer basket in a single layer. Spray lightly with olive oil and air fry at 360ºF (185°C) for 8–10 minutes, until golden and crispy. Repeat with any remaining onions and serve.

Lunch

41. Lemon-Garlic Chicken

Servings| 4   Time| 2 hours 35 minutes
Nutritional Content (per serving):
Cal| Fat| g   Protein| g   Carbs| g

Ingredients:
- ¼ cup (62.5ml) Lemon juice
- 1 Tbsp. olive oil
- 1 tsp mustard
- Cloves of garlic
- ¼ tsp salt
- ⅛ tsp black pepper
- Chicken thighs
- Lemon wedges

Directions:
1. In a bowl, whisk together the olive oil, lemon juice, mustard Dijon, garlic, salt, and pepper.
2. Place the chicken thighs in a large Ziploc bag. Spill marinade over chicken & seal bag, ensuring all chicken parts are covered. Cool for at least 2 hours.
3. Preheat a frying pan to 360°F (185°C). Remove the chicken with towels from the marinade, & pat dry.
4. Place pieces of chicken in the air fryer basket, if necessary, cook them in batches.
5. Fry till chicken is no longer pink on the bone & the juices run smoothly, 22 to 24 min. Upon serving, press a lemon slice across each piece.

42. Herb-Marinated Chicken Thighs

Servings| 4   Time| 45 minutes
Nutritional Content (per serving):
Cal| 100   Fat| 9g   Protein| 5g   Carbs| 1g

Ingredients:
- 8 Chicken thighs, skin-on, bone-in
- 2 tbsp. Lemon juice
- ½ tsp. Onion powder
- 2 tsp. Garlic powder
- 1 tsp. Spike Seasoning
- 55g Olive oil
- 1 tsp. Dried basil
- ½ tsp. Dried oregano
- ¼ tsp Black Pepper

Directions:
1. In a bowl, add dried oregano, olive oil, lemon juice, dried sage, garlic powder, Spike Seasoning, onion powder, dried basil, black pepper.
2. In a Ziploc bag, add the spice blend and the chicken and mix well. Marinate the chicken in the refrigerator for six hours or more.
3. Preheat the air fryer to 360°F (185°C).
4. Put the chicken in the air fryer basket, cook for 6 minutes, flip the chicken, and cook for 6 minutes more.
5. Take out from the air fryer and serve with microgreens.

43. Blackened Chicken Breast

Servings| 2   Time| 30 minutes
Nutritional Content (per serving):
Cal| 431   Fat| 9g   Protein| 80g   Carbs| 3g

Ingredients:
- 2 tsp. Paprika
- 1 tsp. Ground thyme
- 1 tsp. Cumin
- ½ tsp. Cayenne pepper
- ½ tsp. Onion powder
- ½ tsp. Black Pepper
- ¼ tsp Salt
- 2 tsp Vegetable oil
- Pieces of chicken breast halves (without bones and skin)

Directions:
1. In a mixing bowl, add onion powder, salt, cumin, paprika, black pepper, thyme, and cayenne pepper. Mix it well.
2. Drizzle oil over chicken and rub. Dip each piece of chicken in blackening spice blend on both sides.
3. Let it rest for five minutes while the air fryer is preheating. Preheat it for five minutes at 360°F 185°C.
4. Put the chicken in the air fryer and let it cook for ten minutes. Flip and then cook for another ten minutes.
5. After, let it sit for five minutes, then slice and serve with the side of greens.

44. Air Fryer Brown Rice Chicken Fried

Servings| 2   Time| 20 minutes
Nutritional Content (per serving):
Cal| 350   Fat| 6g   Protein| 22g   Carbs| 20g

Ingredients:
- Olive Oil Cooking Spray
- 260g (9oz) Chicken Breast, diced & cooked &
- 25g (1oz) White Onion, chopped
- 65g (2oz) Celery, chopped
- 715g (25oz) Cooked brown rice
- 45g (2oz) Carrots chopped

Directions:
1. Place foil on the air fryer basket, make sure to leave room for air to flow, roll up on the sides.
2. Spray with olive oil. Mix all ingredients and add them on the top of the foil, in the air fryer basket.
3. Give an olive oil spray on the mixture. Cook for five minutes at 390°F (200°C).
4. Open the air fryer and give a toss to the mixture. Cook for five more minutes at 390F (200°C).

45. Chicken Thighs Smothered Style

Servings| 4   Time| 60 minutes
Nutritional Content (per serving):
Cal| 466   Fat| 32g   Protein| 41g   Carbs| 2g

Ingredients:
- 225g (8oz) chicken thighs
- 1 tsp. paprika
- One pinch salt
- 90g (3oz) Mushrooms
- Onions, roughly sliced

Directions:
1. Let the air fryer preheat to 400°F (205°C).
2. Season chicken thighs with paprika, salt, and pepper on both sides.
3. Place the thighs in the air fryer and cook for 20 minutes.
4. Meanwhile, sauté the mushroom and onion.
5. Take out the thighs from the air fryer serve with sautéed mushrooms and onions.

46. Zucchini Turkey Burgers

Servings| 5   Time| 20 minutes
Nutritional Content (per serving):
Cal| 161   Fat| 7g   Protein| 19g   Carbs| 4g

Ingredients:
- 30g (1oz) Gluten-free breadcrumbs
- 180g (6oz) Grated zucchini
- 1 tbsp. Red onion (grated)
- 730g (26oz) Lean ground turkey
- One clove of minced garlic
- 1 tsp of kosher salt and fresh pepper

Directions:
1. In a bowl, add zucchini (moisture removed with a paper towel), ground turkey, garlic, salt, onion, pepper, breadcrumbs. Mix well. With your hands make five patties. But not too thick.
2. Let the air fryer preheat to 375°F (190°C).
3. Put in an air fryer in a single layer and cook for 7 minutes or more. Until cooked through and browned.
4. Place in buns with ketchup and lettuce and enjoy.

47. Air Fryer Hamburgers

Servings| 4   Time| 20 minutes
Nutritional Content (per serving):
Cal| 520   Fat| 34g   Protein| 31g   Carbs| 22g

Ingredients:
- 4 Buns
- 1030g (36oz) Lean ground beef chuck
- Salt to taste
- 4 slices of any cheese
- Black Pepper, to taste

Directions:
1. Let the air fryer preheat to 350°F (180°C).
2. In a bowl, add lean ground beef, pepper, and salt. Mix well and form patties.
3. Put the patties in the air fryer in one layer only, cook for 6 minutes, flip them halfway through.
4. One minute before you take out the patties, add cheese on top. When cheese is melted, take out from the air fryer.
5. Add ketchup, any dressing, tomatoes, lettuce and patties to your buns. Serve hot.

48. Taco-Stuffed Peppers

Servings| 4   Time| 35 minutes
Nutritional Content (per serving):
Cal| 346   Fat| 19g   Protein| 28g   Carbs| 110g

Ingredients:
- 455g (1 lb.) 80/20 ground beef
- 1 tbsp. chili powder
- 2 tsp. cumin
- 1 tsp. garlic powder
- 1 tsp. salt
- 1/4 tsp. ground black pepper
- 1 can (10 oz.) diced tomatoes and green chiles, drained
- 4 medium green bell peppers
- 260g (9oz) shredded Monterey jack cheese, divided

Directions:
1. In a medium skillet over medium heat, brown the ground beef for about 7 minutes. When no pink remains, drain the fat from the skillet.
2. Return the skillet to the stovetop and add chili powder, cumin, garlic powder, salt, and black pepper.
3. Add drained can have diced tomatoes and chiles to the skillet. Continue cooking for 3–5 minutes.
4. While the mixture is cooking, cut each bell pepper in half. Remove the seeds and white membrane.
5. Spoon the cooked mixture evenly into each bell pepper and top with a 65g (2oz) of cheese.
6. Place the stuffed peppers into the air fryer basket. Set the temperature to 350°F (180°C) and cook for 15 minutes.
7. When done, peppers will be fork-tender, and cheese will be browned and bubbling. Serve warm.

49. Flavourful Meatballs

Servings| 6   Time| 40 minutes
Nutritional Content (per serving):
Cal| 204   Fat| 7g   Protein| 27g   Carbs| 7g

Ingredients:
- 200g (7oz) ground beef
- 200g (7oz) ground chicken
- 100g (4oz) ground pork
- 30g (1oz) minced garlic
- 1 potato
- 1 egg
- 1 tsp. basil
- 1 tsp. cayenne pepper
- 1 tsp. white pepper
- 2 tsp. olive oil

Directions:
1. Combine ground beef, chicken meat, and pork in the mixing bowl and stir it gently.
2. Sprinkle it with basil, cayenne pepper, and white pepper.
3. Add minced garlic and egg. Stir the mixture gently. You should get a fluffy mass.
4. Peel the potato and grate it. Add grated potato to the mixture and stir it again.
5. Preheat the air fryer oven to 375°F (190°C). Take a tray and spray it with olive oil.
6. Make the balls from the meat mass and put them on the tray. Lay the tray in the oven and cook it for 25 minutes.

50. Beef with Mushrooms

Servings| 4   Time| 55 minutes
Nutritional Content (per serving):
Cal| 175   Fat| 6g   Protein| 26g   Carbs| 4g

Ingredients:
- 300g (11oz) beef
- 150g (5oz) mushrooms
- 1 onion
- 1 tsp. olive oil
- 1/3 cup (100ml) vegetable broth
- 1 tsp. basil
- 1 tsp. chili
- 2 tbsp. tomato juice

Directions:
1. Take the beef and pierce the meat with a knife. Rub it with olive oil, basil, and chili, and lemon juice.
2. Chop the onion and mushrooms and pour them with vegetable broth. Cook the vegetables for 5 minutes.
3. Take a big tray and put the meat in it. Add vegetable broth to the tray too. It will make the meat juicy.
4. Preheat the air fryer oven to 375ºF (190°C) and cook it for 35 minutes.

51. Lemon Greek Beef and Vegetables

Servings| 4   Time| 25 minutes
Nutritional Content (per serving):
Cal| 98   Fat| 1g   Protein| 16g   Carbs| 5g

Ingredients:
- 230g (½ lb) 96% lean ground beef
- 2 medium tomatoes, chopped
- 1 onion, chopped
- 2 garlic cloves, minced
- 2 cups fresh baby spinach
- 2 tbsp. freshly squeezed lemon juice
- ⅓ cup low-sodium beef broth
- 2 tbsp. crumbled low-sodium feta cheese

Directions:
1. In a baking pan, crumble the beef. Place in the air fryer basket. Air fry at 370ºF (190°C) for 6 minutes, stirring once during cooking until browned. Drain off any fat or liquid.
2. Swell the tomatoes, onion, and garlic into the pan. Air fry for 4 minutes more.
3. Add the spinach, lemon juice, and beef broth.
4. Air fry for 4 minutes more, or until the spinach is wilted.
5. Sprinkle with the feta cheese and serve immediately.

52. Paprika Pulled Pork

Servings| 4   Time| 40 minutes
Nutritional Content (per serving):
Cal| 198   Fat| 6g   Protein| 31g   Carbs| 2g

Ingredients:
- 1 tbsp. chili flakes
- 1 tsp. ground black pepper
- ½ tsp. paprika
- 1 tsp. cayenne pepper
- 80g (3oz) cream
- 1 tsp. kosher salt
- 1-lb. pork tenderloin
- 1 tsp. ground thyme
- 945g (33oz) chicken stock
- 1 tsp. butter

Directions:
1. Pour the chicken stock into the air fryer basket tray.
2. Add the pork steak and sprinkle the mixture with chili flakes, paprika, cayenne pepper, ground black pepper, and salt. Preheat the air fryer to 370°F (190°C) and cook the meat for 20 minutes.
3. Strain the liquid and shred the meat with 2 forks.
4. Then add the butter and cream and mix it.
5. Cook the pulled pork for 4 minutes more at 360°F (185°C). When the pulled pork is cooked allow to rest briefly.

53. Air Fryer Pork Chop & Broccoli

Servings| 2   Time| 30 minutes
Nutritional Content (per serving):
Cal| 483   Fat| 20g   Protein| 24g   Carbs| 12g

Ingredients:
- 365g (13oz) Broccoli florets
- 2 pieces Bone-in pork chop
- ½ tsp. Paprika
- 2 tbsp. Avocado oil
- ½ tsp. Garlic powder
- ½ tsp. Onion powder
- Two cloves of crushed garlic
- 1 tsp. Salt, divided

Directions:
1. Let the air fryer preheat to 350°F (180°C). Spray the basket with cooking oil.
2. Add 1 tbsp. Oil, garlic powder, onion powder, half tsp. of salt, and paprika in a bowl and mix well. Rub this spice mix to the pork chop's sides.
3. Add pork chops to air fryer basket and cook for five minutes.
4. In the meantime, add one tsp. oil, garlic, half tsp of salt, and broccoli to a bowl and coat well.
5. Flip the pork chop, add the broccoli, and cook for five more minutes.
6. Take out from the air fryer and serve.

54. Cheesy Pork Chops in Air Fryer

Servings| 2   Time| 13 minutes
Nutritional Content (per serving):
Cal| 467   Fat| 22g   Protein| 62g   Carbs| 10g

Ingredients:
- 4 lean pork chops
- ½ tsp. Salt
- ½ tsp. Garlic powder
- 4 tbsp. shredded cheese
- Chopped cilantro

Directions:
1. Let the air fryer preheat to 350°F (180°C). Rub the pork chops with garlic, cilantro, and salt. Put in the air fryer and let it cook for four minutes.
2. Flip them and cook for two minutes more.
3. Add cheese on top and cook for another two minutes or until the cheese is melted. Serve with salad greens.

55. Pork Trinova Wrapped in Ham

Servings| 6   Time| 17 minutes
Nutritional Content (per serving):
Cal| 282   Fat| 23g   Protein| 17g   Carbs| 0g

Ingredients:
- 6 pieces Serrano ham, thinly sliced
- 454g. (16oz) pork, halved, with butter and crushed
- 5g. (0.2oz) salt
- 1g. (0.04 oz) black pepper
- 230g. (8oz) fresh spinach leaves, divided
- 4 slices Mozzarella cheese, divided
- 20g. (0.3oz) sun-dried tomatoes, divided
- 2 tbsp. olive oil, divided

Directions:
1. Place 3 pieces of ham on baking paper, slightly overlapping each other. Place 1 half of the pork in the ham. Repeat with the other half. Season the inside of the pork rolls with salt and pepper.
2. Place half of the spinach, cheese, and sun-dried tomatoes on top of the pork loin, leaving a 13 mm. border on all sides.
3. Roll the fillet around the filling and tie it with a kitchen cord to keep it closed.
4. Repeat the process for the other pork steak and place them in the fridge.
5. Warm in the air fryer and press START/PAUSE.
6. Brush the olive oil on each wrapped steak and place them in the preheated air fryer.
7. Select STEAK. Set the timer to 9 minutes and press START/PAUSE. Let it cool before cutting.

56. Stuffed Cabbage and Pork Loin Rolls

Servings| 4   Time| 25 minutes
Nutritional Content (per serving):
Cal| 120   Fat| 3g   Protein| 21g   Carbs| 0g

Ingredients:
- 500g. (18oz) white cabbage
- 1 onion
- 8 pork tenderloin steaks
- 2 carrots
- 4 tbsp. soy sauce
- 50g. (2oz) extra virgin olive oil
- Salt to taste
- 8 sheets rice

Directions:
1. Put the chopped cabbage in the Thermo mix glass together with the onion and the chopped carrot.
2. Select 5 seconds on the speed 5. Add the extra virgin olive oil. Select 5 minutes, left turn, and spoon speed.
3. Cut the tenderloin steaks into thin strips. Add the meat to the thermo mix glass. Select 5 minutes, room temperature, left turn, spoon speed without beaker.
4. Add the soy sauce. Select 5 minutes, room temperature, left turn, spoon speed. Rectify salt. Let it cold down.
5. Hydrate the rice slices. Extend and distribute the filling between them.
6. Make the rolls, folding so that the edges are completely closed. Set the rolls in the air fryer and paint with the oil.
7. Select 10 minutes for cooking time and set the temperature to 375°F (190°C).

57. Asian Sesame Cod

Servings| 1   Time| 15 minutes
Nutritional Content (per serving):
Cal| 140   Fat| 1g   Protein| 27g   Carbs| 7g

Ingredients:
- 1 tbsp. reduced-sodium soy sauce
- 2 tsp. honey
- 1 tsp. sesame seeds
- 170g (6oz) cod fillet

Directions:
1. In a lesser bowl, syndicate the soy sauce and honey.
2. Sprig the air fryer basket with non-stick cooking spray, then place the fish in the basket, brush with the soy mixture, and sprinkle with sesame seeds. Roast at 360°F (185°C) for 10 minutes or until opaque.
3. Remove the fryer's fish and allow cooling on a wire rack for 5 minutes before serving.

58. Sriracha Calamari

Servings| 2   Time| 25 minutes
Nutritional Content (per serving):
Cal| 252   Fat| 39g   Protein| 42g   Carbs| 3g

Ingredients:
- 240g (8oz) Club soda
- 1-2 tbsp. Sriracha
- 450g (16oz) Calamari tubes
- 125g (4oz) Flour
- Pinches of salt
- freshly ground black pepper
- red pepper flakes

Directions:
1. Cut the calamari tubes into rings. Submerge them with club soda. Let it rest for ten minutes.
2. In the meantime, in a bowl, add freshly ground black pepper, flour, red pepper, and kosher salt and mix well.
3. Drain the calamari and pat dry with a paper towel. Coat well the calamari in the flour mix and set aside.
4. Spray oil in the air fryer basket and put calamari in one single layer.
5. Cook at 375°F (190°C) for 11 minutes. Toss the rings twice while cooking.
6. Meanwhile, to make sauce, add red pepper flakes, and sriracha in a bowl, mix well.
7. Take calamari out from the basket, mix with sauce and cook for another two minutes more. Serve with salad green.

59. Shrimp Rolls in Air Fryer

Servings| 4 Time| 20 minutes
Nutritional Content (per serving):
Cal| 180   Fat| 9g   Protein| 18g   Carbs| 9g

Ingredients:
- 90g (3oz) deveined raw shrimp, chopped, peeled
- 2 ½ tbsp. Olive oil
- 180g (6oz) Matchstick carrots
- 115g (4oz) slices of red bell pepper
- ¼ tsp. red pepper (crushed)
- 90g (3oz) snow peas, slices
- 365g (13oz) cabbage, shredded
- 1 tbsp. Lime juice
- ½ cup (125ml) Sweet chili sauce
- 2 tsp. Fish sauce
- Eight spring rolls (wrappers)

Directions:
1. In a skillet, add one and a half tbsp. of olive, until smoking lightly. Stir in bell pepper, cabbage, carrots, and cook for two minutes. Turn off the heat, take out in a dish and cool for five minutes.
2. In a bowl, add shrimp, lime juice, cabbage mixture, crushed red pepper, fish sauce, and snow peas. Mix well
3. Lay spring roll wrappers on a plate. Add 40g (1oz) of filling in the middle of each wrapper. Fold tightly with water. Brush the olive oil over folded rolls.
4. Put spring rolls in the air fryer basket and cook for 6 to 7 minutes at 390°F (200°C) until light brown and crispy.
5. You may serve with sweet chili sauce.

60. Lime-Garlic Shrimp Kebabs

Servings| 2   Time| 13 minutes
Nutritional Content (per serving):
Cal| 75   Fat| 9g   Protein| 14g   Carbs| 4g

Ingredients:
- One lime
- 180g (6oz) Raw shrimp
- 1/8 tsp. Salt
- 1 clove of garlic
- Freshly ground black pepper

Directions:
1. In water, let wooden skewers soak for 20 minutes.
2. Let the Air fryer preheat to 350°F (180°C).
3. In a bowl, mix shrimp, minced garlic, lime juice, kosher salt, and pepper.
4. Add shrimp on skewers. Place skewers in the air fryer and cook for 8 minutes. Turn halfway over.

61. Fish Finger Sandwich

Servings| 3   Time| 25 minutes
Nutritional Content (per serving):
Cal| 240   Fat| 12g   Protein| 21g   Carbs| 7g

Ingredients:
- 1 tbsp. Greek yogurt
- 4 Cod fillets, without skin
- 2 tbsp. Flour
- 5 tbsp. Whole-wheat breadcrumbs
- Kosher salt and pepper to taste
- 10–12 Capers
- 100g (3oz) Frozen peas
- Lemon juice

Directions:
1. Let the air fryer preheat.
2. Sprinkle kosher salt and pepper on the cod fillets, and coat in flour, then in breadcrumbs.
3. Spray the fryer basket with oil. Put the cod fillets in the basket. Cook for 15 minutes at 400°F (205°C).
4. Meanwhile, cook the peas in boiling water for a few minutes. Take out from the water and blend with Greek yogurt, lemon juice, and capers until well combined.
5. On a bun, add cooked fish with pea puree. Add lettuce and tomato.

Dinner

62. Catfish with Green Beans, in Southern Style

Servings| 2   Time| 30 minutes

Nutritional Content (per serving):
Cal| 243   Fat| 18g   Protein| 34g   Carbs| 18g

Ingredients:
- 2 pieces Catfish fillets
- 60g (2oz) Green beans, trimmed
- Freshly ground black pepper and salt, to taste divided
- ½ tsp. Crushed red pepper
- 65g (2oz) Flour
- One egg, lightly beaten
- ¾ tsp. Dill pickle relish
- ½ tsp. Apple cider vinegar
- 35g (1oz) whole-wheat breadcrumbs
- 2 tbsp. Mayonnaise
- Dill
- Lemon wedges

Directions:
1. In a bowl, add green beans, spray them with cooking oil. Coat with crushed red pepper, 1/8 tsp. of kosher salt, and half tsp. of honey and cook in the air fryer at 400°F (205°C) until soft and browned, for 12 minutes. Take out from fryer and cover with aluminium foil.
2. In the meantime, coat catfish in flour. Then dip in egg to coat, then in breadcrumbs. Place fish in an air fryer basket and spray with cooking oil.
3. Cook for 8 minutes, at 400°F (205°C), until cooked through and golden brown.
4. Sprinkle with pepper and salt. In the meantime, mix vinegar, dill, relish, mayonnaise, in a bowl. Serve the sauce with fish and green beans.

63. Parmesan Garlic Crusted Salmon

Servings| 2   Time| 20 minutes
Nutritional Content (per serving):
Cal| 340   Fat| 19g   Protein| 32g   Carbs| 7g

Ingredients:
- 25g (1oz) whole-wheat breadcrumbs
- 730g (25oz) salmon
- 1 tbsp. butter, melted
- 1/4 tsp. freshly ground black pepper
- 65g (2oz) Parmesan cheese, grated
- 2 tsp. garlic, minced
- 1/2 tsp. Italian seasoning

Directions:
1. Let the air fryer preheat to 400°F (205°C), spray the oil over the air fryer basket.
2. Pat the salmon dry.
3. In a bowl, mix Parmesan cheese, Italian seasoning, and breadcrumbs. In another pan, mix melted butter with garlic and add to the breadcrumbs mix. Mix well.
4. Add kosher salt and freshly ground black pepper to salmon. On top of every salmon piece, add the crust mix and press gently.
5. Let the air fryer preheat to 400°F (205°C) and add salmon to it. Cook until done to your liking (about 15 minutes).
6. Serve hot with vegetable side dishes.

64. Air Fried Cajun Salmon

Servings| 1   Time| 20 minutes
Nutritional Content (per serving):
Cal| 215   Fat| 19g   Protein| 20g   Carbs| 1g

Ingredients:
- 1 fresh salmon
- 1 tbsp. Cajun seasoning
- 1 lemon juice

Directions:
1. Let the air fryer preheat to 375°F (190°C). Pat dries the salmon fillet. Rub lemon juice and Cajun seasoning over the fish fillet.
2. Place in the air fryer and cook for 7 minutes.

65. Lime Baked Salmon

Servings| 2   Time| 22 minutes
Nutritional Content (per serving):
Cal| 167   Fat| 9g   Protein| 19g   Carbs| 6g

Ingredients:
- 2 (3 oz.) salmon fillets, skin removed
- 40g () jalapeños, sliced and pickled
- 1/2 medium lime, juiced
- 2 tbsp. cilantro, chopped
- 1 tbsp. salted butter; melted.
- 1/2tsp. garlic, finely minced
- 1 tsp. chili powder

Directions:
1. Place the salmon fillets into a 6-inch round baking pan. Brush each with butter and sprinkle with chili powder and garlic.
2. Place the jalapeño slices on top and around salmon.
3. Pour half of the lime juice over the salmon and cover with foil. Place pan into the air fryer basket.
4. Adjust the temperature to 370ºF (190°C) and set the timer for 12 minutes.
5. The internal temperature of salmon should reach at least 145°F (65°C) after it is fully cooked.
6. Garnish with cilantro and spritz with the remaining lime juice.

66. Cajun Salmon

Servings| 2   Time| 12 minutes
Nutritional Content (per serving):
Cal| 253   Fat| 16g   Protein| 30g   Carbs| 4g

Ingredients:
- 2 (4 oz.) salmon fillets, skin removed
- 2 tbsp. unsalted butter, melted.
- 1 tsp. paprika
- 1/4 tsp. ground black pepper
- 1/8 tsp. ground cayenne pepper
- 1/2 tsp. garlic powder.

Directions:
1. Brush each fillet with butter.
2. Combine the remaining ingredients in a small bowl and then rub them onto the fish.
3. Place the fillets into the air fryer basket.
4. Bring the temperature to 390ºF (200°C) and set the timer for 7 minutes. When fully cooked, the internal temperature will be 145ºF (65°C). Serve immediately.

67. Chicken Pie

Servings| 2   Time| 40 minutes
Nutritional Content (per serving):
Cal| 224   Fat| 18g   Protein| 21g   Carbs| 16g

Ingredients:
- 2 sheets Puff pastry
- 2 pieces Chicken thighs, cut into cubes
- One small onion, chopped
- 2 Small potatoes, chopped
- 45g (2oz) Mushrooms
- Light soya sauce
- One carrot, chopped
- Black pepper to taste
- Worcestershire sauce, to taste
- Salt to taste
- Italian mixed dried herbs
- Garlic powder, a pinch
- 2 tbsp. Plain flour
- Milk, as required
- Melted butter

Directions:
1. In a mixing bowl, add light soya sauce and pepper add the chicken cubes, and coat well.
2. In a pan over medium heat, sauté potatoes, carrot, and onion. Add some water, if required, to cook the vegetables. Add the chicken cubes and mushrooms and cook them too.
3. Stir in black pepper, salt, Worcestershire sauce, garlic powder, and dried herbs.
4. When the chicken is cooked through, add some of the flour and mix well.
5. Add in the milk and let the vegetables simmer until tender.
6. Place one piece of puff pastry in the baking tray of the air fryer, poke holes with a fork.
7. Add on top the cooked chicken filling and eggs and puff pastry on top with holes. Cut the excess pastry off. Glaze with melted butter.
8. Air fry at 180°F (85°C) for six minutes, or until it becomes golden brown.
9. Serve right away and enjoy.

68. Air Fryer Brown Rice Chicken Fried

Servings| 2   Time| 20 minutes
Nutritional Content (per serving):
Cal| 350   Fat| 6g   Protein| 22g   Carbs| 20g

Ingredients:
- Olive Oil Cooking Spray
- 180g (6oz) Chicken Breast, Diced & Cooked &
- 45g (2oz) White Onion, chopped
- 40g (2oz) Celery, chopped
- 545g (19oz) Cooked brown rice
- 45g (2oz) Carrots, chopped

Directions:
1. Place foil on the air fryer basket, make sure to leave room for air to flow, roll up on the sides.
2. Spray with olive oil. Mix all ingredient s and add them on the top of the foil, in the air fryer basket.
3. Give an olive oil spray on the mixture. Cook for five minutes at 390°F (200°C).
4. Open the air fryer and give a toss to the mixture. Cook for five more minutes at 390°F (200°C).

69. Buttermilk Chicken in Air-Fryer

Servings| 6   Time| 50 minutes
Nutritional Content (per serving):
Cal| 210   Fat| 18g   Protein| 23g   Carbs| 12g

Ingredients:
- 730g (26oz) Chicken thighs, skin-on, bone-in

Marinade:
- 490g (17oz) Buttermilk
- 2 tsp. Black pepper
- 1 tsp. Cayenne pepper
- 2 tsp. Salt

Seasoned Flour:
- 1 tbsp. Baking powder
- 250g (9oz) All-purpose flour
- 1 tbsp. Paprika powder
- 1 tsp. Salt
- 1 tbsp. Garlic powder

Directions:
1. Let the air fry heat at 356°F (180°C). With a paper towel, pat dry the chicken thighs.
2. In a mixing bowl, add paprika, black pepper, salt mix well, then add chicken pieces. Add buttermilk and coat the chicken well. Let it marinate for at least 6 hours.
3. In another bowl, add baking powder, salt, flour, pepper, and paprika. Put one by one of the chicken pieces and coat in the seasoning mix.
4. Spray oil on chicken pieces and place breaded chicken skin side up in air fryer basket in one layer, cook for 8 minutes, then flip the chicken pieces' cook for another ten minutes.

70. Chicken with Mixed Vegetables

Servings| 2   Time| 20 minutes
Nutritional Content (per serving):
Cal| 230   Fat| 8g   Protein| 27g   Carbs| 8g

Ingredients:
- 1/2 onion diced
- 730g (26oz) Chicken breast, cubed pieces
- Half zucchini chopped
- 1 tbsp. Italian seasoning
- 75g (3oz) Bell pepper chopped
- Clove of garlic pressed
- 75g (3oz) Broccoli florets
- 2 tbsps. Olive oil
- ½ tsp. of chili powder, garlic powder, pepper, salt

Directions:
1. Let the air fryer heat to 400°F (205°C) and dice the vegetables. In a bowl, add the seasoning, oil and add vegetables, chicken and toss well.
2. Place chicken and vegetables in the air fryer, and cook for ten minutes, toss halfway through, cook in batches.
3. Make sure the veggies are charred and the chicken is cooked through. Serve hot.

71. Lemon Rosemary Chicken

Servings| 2   Time| 50 minutes
Nutritional Content (per serving):
Cal| 308   Fat| 12g   Protein| 26g   Carbs| 7g

Ingredients:

For marinade:
- 455g (16oz) Chicken
- 1 tsp. Ginger, minced
- 1/2 tbsp. Olive oil
- 1 tbsp. Soy sauce

For the sauce:
- Half lemon
- Honey
- 1 tbsp. Oyster sauce
- 142g (5oz) Fresh rosemary, chopped

Directions:
1. In a big mixing bowl, add the marinade ingredients with chicken, and mix well.
2. Keep in the refrigerator for at least half an hour.
3. Let the oven preheat to 392°F (200°C) for three minutes.
4. Place the marinated chicken in the air fryer in a single layer. And cook for 6 minutes at 392°F (200°C).
5. Meanwhile, add all the sauces ingredients in a bowl and mix well except for lemon wedges.
6. Brush the sauce generously over half-baked chicken. Add lemon juice on top.
7. Cook for another 13 minutes at 392°F (200°C). flip the chicken halfway through. Let the chicken evenly brown.

72. Air Fried Steak with Asparagus

Servings| 2   Time| 50 minutes
Nutritional Content (per serving):
Cal| 470   Fat| 15g   Protein| 30g   Carbs| 20g

Ingredients:
- Olive oil spray
- 910g (2 lbs) Flank steak, cut into 6 pieces
- Kosher salt and black pepper
- Two cloves of minced garlic
- 730g (26oz) Asparagus
- ½ cup (120ml) Tamari sauce
- Three bell peppers, sliced thinly
- 1/3 cup (79ml) Beef broth
- 1 Tbsp. of unsalted butter
- ¼ cup (60ml) Balsamic vinegar

Directions:
1. Sprinkle salt and pepper on steak and rub. In a Ziploc bag, add Tamari sauce and garlic, then add steak, toss well and seal the bag.
2. Let it marinate for one hour to overnight. Place asparagus and bell peppers in the centre of the steak.
3. Roll the steak around the vegetables and close it well with toothpicks.
4. Preheat the air fryer. Spray the steak with olive oil spray. And place steaks in the air fryer.
5. Cook for 15 minutes at 400°F (205°C). Remove the steak from the air fryer and let it rest for five minutes before slicing.
6. In the meantime, add balsamic vinegar, butter, and broth over medium flame. Mix well and reduce it by half.
7. Add salt and pepper to taste. Pour over steaks right before serving.

73. Air Fry Rib-Eye Steak

Servings| 2   Time| 20minutes
Nutritional Content (per serving):
Cal| 469   Fat| 30g   Protein| 46g   Carbs| 23g

Ingredients:
- 2 medium-sized Lean rib eye steaks
- Salt & freshly ground black pepper, to taste

Directions:
1. Let the air fry preheat at 400°F (205°C).
2. Season the meat with salt and pepper and put in the air fryer basket. Cook for 14 minutes and flip after half time.
3. Take out from the air fryer and let it rest for 5 minutes. Serve with microgreen salad.

74. Beef and Ale Casserole

Servings| 4   Time| 1 hour 10 minutes
Nutritional Content (per serving):
Cal| 604   Fat| 22g   Protein| 59g   Carbs| 33g

Ingredients:
- Three tbsps. plain flour
- 680g (1 ½ lbs) leg of beef or diced braising steak
- Three tbsps. of olive oil
- Two medium onions, cut into big wedges
- 370g (13oz) carrots, cut into big chunks
- 200g (7oz)parsnip, cut into large chunks
- 2 cups (475ml) strong ale
- Three tbsps. fresh thyme
- One bay leaf

Directions:
1. Heat the oven to 340°F (170°C). Spread the flour on a dinner plate. Add beef in the flour.
2. Pour two tsp of oil into a big frying pan. Fry beef on medium heat for 2-3 minutes.
3. Fry until each side is brown all over. Shift the meat onto a plate and set aside.
4. Continue following the above instructions with the remaining meat. You can add more oil if required.
5. Put the remaining oil in a frying pan. Heat it moderately and sauté the onions, carrots, and parsnips for five minutes.
6. Then put the beef and vegetables into an ovenproof casserole dish. Pour in the ale, sprinkle the thyme and bay leaf.
7. Cover with a lid. Cook in the oven for an hour. Wait till it is properly cooked. Serve immediately.

75. Meatloaf

Servings| 8   Time| 55 minutes
Nutritional Content (per serving):
Cal| 330   Fat| 10g   Protein| 19g   Carbs| 16g

Ingredients:
- 730g (26oz) ground lean beef
- 110g (4oz) breadcrumbs, soft and fresh
- 90g (3oz) mushrooms, chopped
- 3 garlic cloves, minced
- 90g (3oz) carrots, shredded
- 45g (2oz) beef broth
- 90g (3oz) onions, chopped
- 2 eggs beaten
- 3 tbsp. ketchup
- 1 tbsp. Worcestershire sauce
- 1 tbsp. Dijon mustard

For the glaze:
- ¼ cup (60ml) honey
- ½ cup (118ml) ketchup
- 2 tsp. Dijon mustard

Directions:
1. In a big bowl, add the beef broth and breadcrumbs; stir well. Set it aside in a food processor, add garlic, onions, mushrooms, and carrots, and pulse on HIGH until finely chopped.
2. Add soaked breadcrumbs, Dijon mustard, Worcestershire sauce, eggs, lean ground beef, ketchup, and salt in a separate bowl. With your hands, combine well and make it into a loaf.
3. Let the air fryer preheat to 390ºF (200ºC). Put the meatloaf in the oven and let it cook for 45 minutes.
4. In the meantime, add Dijon mustard, ketchup, and brown sugar to a bowl and mix. Glaze this mix over the meatloaf when 5 minutes are left.
5. Let it cool for 10 minutes before serving.

76. Lamb Chops with Herb Butter

Servings| 4   Time|15 minutes
Nutritional Content (per serving):
Cal| 278   Fat| 12g   Protein| 39g   Carbs| 0g

Ingredients:
- 4 lamb chops
- 1 tsp. rosemary, diced
- 1 tbsp. butter
- Pepper
- Salt

Directions:
1. Season lamb chops with pepper and salt. Place the dehydrating tray in a multi-level air fryer basket. Insert the basket in the air fryer oven.
2. Place the lamb chops on dehydrating tray. Seal pot with the air fryer lid and select "Air Fry" mode, then set the temperature to 400ºF (205°C) and cook for 5 minutes.
3. Stir in rosemary and butter and spread overcooked lamb chops. Serve and enjoy.

77. Jamaican Jerk Pork

Servings| 4   Time| 30 minutes
Nutritional Content (per serving):
Cal| 234   Fat| 9g   Protein| 32g   Carbs| 11g

Ingredients:
- Pork, cut into three-inch pieces
- 60g (2oz) Jerk paste

Directions:
1. Rub jerk paste all over the pork pieces. Let it marinate for four hours in the refrigerator.
2. Let the air fryer preheat to 390°F (200°C). spray with olive oil.
3. Before putting in the air fryer, let the meat sit for 20 minutes at room temperature.
4. Cook for 20 minutes at 390°F (200°C) in the air fryer, flip halfway through.
5. Take out from the air fryer and let it rest for ten minutes before slicing. Serve with microgreens.

78. 12-Minute Pork Loin

Servings| 4   Time| 25 minutes
Nutritional Content (per serving):
Cal| 175   Fat| 10g   Protein| 17g   Carbs| 1g

Ingredients:
- 1 tbsp. water
- 1 tbsp. Worcestershire sauce
- 1 tbsp. lemon juice
- 1 tbsp. Dijon-style mustard
- 4 boneless pork top loin chops
- ½ tbsp. lemon-pepper seasoning
- 1 tbsp. butter
- 1 tbsp. snipped fresh chives

Directions:
1. For the sauce, combine water, Worcestershire sauce, lemon juice, and mustard in a small bowl; set aside.
2. Trim fat from chops. Use the lemon-pepper seasoning to sprinkle both sides of each chop.
3. In a 10-inch pan, melt butter over medium heat. Add chops and cook for 12 minutes. Rotating once halfway through the cooking period.
4. Withdraw from the heat. Place chops to a serving plate; protect and hold warm.
5. Pour the sauce into the pan; stir and extract any crusty brown pieces from the bottom of the pan. Pour the gravy over the chops. Sprinkle chives.

79. Spiced Pork Chops

Servings| 2   Time| 20 minutes
Nutritional Content (per serving):
Cal| 118   Fat| 6g   Protein| 14g   Carbs| 0g

Ingredients:
- 2 pork chops, boneless
- 0.1cup (15ml) vegetable oil
- 25g (1oz) dark brown sugar, packaged
- 5g (0.2oz) Hungarian paprika
- 2½ g (0.1oz) ground mustard
- 2g (0.1oz) freshly ground black pepper
- 5g (0.1oz) onion powder
- 5g (0.1oz) garlic powder
- Salt and pepper to taste

Directions:
1. Warm the air fryer for a few minutes at 375°F (190°C). Cover the pork chops with oil.
2. Put all the spices and season the pork chops abundantly, almost as if you were making them breaded.
3. Place the pork chops in the preheated air fryer. Select STEAK and set the time to 10 minutes. Remove the pork chops when it has finished cooking.
4. Let it stand and serve.

80. Herbed Pork Ribs

Servings| 4   Time| 26 minutes
Nutritional Content (per serving):
Cal| 296   Fat| 3g   Protein| 30g   Carbs| 6g

Ingredients:
- 500g (18oz) pork ribs
- 1 tbsp. Provencal herbs
- Salt to taste
- Ground pepper to taste
- 1 tsp. oil

Directions:
1. Set the ribs in a bowl and add some oil, Provencal herbs, salt, and ground pepper.
2. Stir well and leave in the fridge for 1 hour.
3. Put the ribs in the basket of the air fryer and select 380°F (195°C) for 20 minutes.
4. From time to time, shake the basket and remove the ribs.

81. Pork Ribs

Servings| 4   Time| 30 minutes
Nutritional Content (per serving):
Cal| 578   Fat| 44g   Protein| 41g   Carbs| 4g

Ingredients:
- 12 pork ribs, trimmed excess fat
- 2 tbsp. corn-starch
- 2 tbsp. olive oil
- 1 tsp. dry mustard
- ½ tsp. thyme
- ½ tsp. garlic powder
- 1 tsp. dried marjoram
- Pinch salt
- Freshly ground black pepper, to taste

Directions:
1. Place the ribs on a clean work surface.
2. In a bowl, combine the olive oil, garlic powder, mustard, corn-starch, thyme, marjoram, salt, and pepper. Rub into the ribs.
3. Place the ribs in the air fryer basket and roast at 400ºF (205°C) for 10 minutes.
4. Turn the ribs with tongs and roast for 10 minutes.

Desserts

82. Cheesecake Bites

Servings| 4   Time| 50 minutes
Nutritional Content (per serving):
Cal| 198   Fat| 18g   Protein| 3g   Carbs| 6g

Ingredients:
- 50g () almond flour
- 2 tbsps. erythritol sweeteners plus ½ cup (118ml), divided
- 230g (8oz) cream cheese, reduced fat, softened
- 1/2 tsp. vanilla extract, unsweetened
- 4 tbsps. heavy cream, reduced fat, divided

Directions:
1. Prepare the cheesecake mixture, and for this, place softened cream cheese in a bowl, add cream, vanilla, and ½ (118g)cup sweetener and whisk using an electric mixer until smooth.
2. Scoop the mixture on a baking sheet lined with parchment sheet, then place it in the freezer for 30 minutes until firm.
3. Place flour in a small bowl and stir in the remaining sweetener.
4. Then switch on the air fryer, insert the fryer basket, grease it with olive oil, then shut with its lid, set the fryer at 350°F (180°C), and preheat for 5 minutes.
5. Meanwhile, cut the cheesecake mix into bite-size pieces and then coat it with an almond flour mixture.
6. Open the fryer, add cheesecake bites in it, close with its lid, and cook for 2 minutes until nicely golden and crispy.
7. Serve straight away.

83. Coconut Pie

Servings| 6   Time| 50 minutes
Nutritional Content (per serving):
Cal| 236   Fat| 16g   Protein| 3g   Carbs| 16g

Ingredients:
- 50g coconut flour
- ½ cup (118ml) erythritol sweetener
- 1 cup shredded coconut, unsweetened, divided
- 1/4 cup butter, unsalted
- 1 1/2 tsp. vanilla extract, unsweetened
- 2 eggs, pastured
- 1 1/2 cups milk, low-fat, unsweetened
- 1/4 cup shredded coconut, toasted

Directions:
1. Switch on the air fryer, insert fryer basket, grease it with olive oil, then shut with its lid, set the fryer at 350°F (180°C), and preheat for 5 minutes.
2. Meanwhile, place all the ingredients in a bowl and whisk until well blended and smooth batter comes together.
3. Take a 6-inches pie pan, grease it with oil, then pour in the prepared batter and smooth the top.
4. Open the fryer, place the pie pan in it, close with its lid, and cook for 45 minutes until pie has set and inserted a toothpick into the pie slide out clean.
5. When the air fryer beeps, open its lid, take out the pie pan and let it cool.
6. Garnish the pie with toasted coconut then cut into slices and serve.

84. Crustless Cheesecake

Servings| 2   Time| 15 minutes
Nutritional Content (per serving):
Cal| 318   Fat| 30g   Protein| 12g   Carbs| 1g

Ingredients:
- 455g (16oz) cream cheese, reduced fat, softened
- 2 tbsps. sour cream, reduced fat
- ¾ cup (118ml) erythritol sweetener
- 1 tsp. vanilla extract, unsweetened
- 2 eggs, pastured
- 1/2 tsp. lemon juice

Directions:
1. Switch on the air fryer, insert fryer basket, grease it with olive oil, then shut with its lid, set the fryer at 350°F (180°C), and preheat for 5 minutes.
2. Meanwhile, take two 4 inches of springform pans, grease them with oil, and set them aside.
3. Crack the eggs in a bowl and then whisk in lemon juice, sweetener, and vanilla until smooth.
4. Whisk in cream cheese and sour cream until blended, divide the mixture evenly between prepared pans.
5. Open the fryer, place pans in it, close with its lid, and cook for 10 minutes until cakes are set and inserted skewer into the cakes slide out clean.
6. When air fryer beeps, open its lid, take out the cake pans and let cakes cool in them.
7. Take out the cakes, refrigerate for 3 hours until cooled, and then serve.

85. Chocolate Cake

Servings| 6   Time| 20 minutes
Nutritional Content (per serving):
Cal| 192   Fat| 16g   Protein| 4g   Carbs| 8g

Ingredients:
- 25g (1oz) coconut flour
- 1 tsp. baking powder
- 35g (1oz) Truvia sweetener
- 1/4 tsp. salt
- 2 tbsp. cocoa powder, unsweetened
- 1 tsp. vanilla extract, unsweetened
- 4 tbsps. butter, unsalted, melted
- 3 eggs, pastured
- 120g (4oz) heavy whipping cream, reduced fat

Directions:
1. Switch on the air fryer, insert fryer basket, grease it with olive oil, then shut with its lid, set the fryer at 350°F (180°C), and preheat for 5 minutes.
2. Meanwhile, take a 6 cups muffin pan, grease it with oil, and set aside until required.
3. Place melted butter in a bowl, whisk in sweetener until blended, and then beat in vanilla, eggs, and cream until combined.
4. Add remaining ingredients, beat again until incorporated and smooth batter comes together, and then pour the mixture into the prepared pan.
5. Open the fryer, place the pan in it, close with its lid, and cook for 10 minutes until the cake is done and inserted skewer into the cake slides out clean.
6. When air fryer beeps, open its lid, take out the cake pan and let the cake cool in it.
7. Take out the cakes, cut them into pieces, and serve.

86. Chocolate Brownies

Servings| 4   Time| 55 minutes
Nutritional Content (per serving):
Cal| 224   Fat| 23g   Protein| 4g   Carbs| 3g

Ingredients:
- 85g (3oz) chocolate chips, sugar-free
- 1 tsp. vanilla extract, unsweetened
- ¼ cup (60ml) erythritol sweetener
- 115g (4oz) butter, unsalted
- 3 eggs, pastured

Directions:
1. Switch on the air fryer, insert fryer basket, grease it with olive oil, then shut with its lid, set the fryer at 350°F (180°C), and preheat for 10 minutes.
2. Add butter and chocolate in a microwaveable bowl and set for 1 minute or until chocolate has melted, stirring every 30 seconds.
3. Crack eggs in another bowl, beat in vanilla and sweetener until smooth and then slowly beat in melted chocolate mixture until well incorporated.
4. Take a springform pan that fits into the air fryer, grease it with oil and then pour in batter in it.
5. Open the fryer, place the pan in it, close with its lid and cook for 35 minutes until cake is done and inserted toothpick into the brownies slide out clean.
6. When air fryer beeps, open its lid, take out the pan and let the brownies cool in it.
7. Then take out the brownies, cut it into even pieces, and serve.

87. Spiced Apples

Servings| 4   Time| 25 minutes
Nutritional Content (per serving):
Cal| 90   Fat| 2g   Protein| 1g   Carbs| 22g

Ingredients:
- 4 small apples, cored, sliced
- 2 tbsps. erythritol sweeteners
- 1 tsp. apple pie spice
- 2 tbsps. olive oil

Directions:
1. Switch on the air fryer, insert fryer basket, grease it with olive oil, then shut with its lid, set the fryer at 350°F (180°C), and preheat for 5 minutes.
2. Meanwhile, place apple slices in a bowl, sprinkle with sweetener and spice, and drizzle with oil and stir until evenly coated.
3. Open the fryer, add apple slices in it, close with its lid and cook for 12 minutes until nicely golden and crispy, shaking halfway through the frying.
4. Serve straight away.

88. Chocolate Lava Cake

Servings| 2   Time| 20 minutes
Nutritional Content (per serving):
Cal| 363   Fat| 34g   Protein| 12g   Carbs| 3g

Ingredients:
- 1 tbsp. flax meal
- 1/2 tsp. baking powder
- 2 tbsps. cocoa powder, unsweetened
- 2 tbsps. erythritol sweeteners
- 1/8 tsp. Stevia sweetener
- 1/8 tsp. vanilla extract, unsweetened
- 1 tbsp. olive oil
- 2 tbsps. water
- 1 egg, pastured

Directions:
1. Switch on the air fryer, insert fryer basket, grease it with olive oil, then shut with its lid, set the fryer at 350°F (180°C), and preheat for 5 minutes.
2. Meanwhile, take a two cups ramekin, grease it with oil and set aside.
3. Get a small bowl and put all ingredients. Mix until well combined and incorporated. Pour the batter into the ramekin.
4. Open the fryer, place ramekin in it, close with its lid and cook for 8 minutes until cake is done and inserted skewer into the cake slides out clean.
5. When air fryer beeps, open its lid, take out the ramekin and let the cake cool in it.
6. Then take out the cake, cut it into slices, and serve.

89. Pecan Pie Bread Pudding

Servings| 4   Time| 25 minutes
Nutritional Content (per serving):
Cal| 290   Fat| 25g   Protein| 3g   Carbs| 16g

Ingredients:
- 260g (9oz) cubes gluten-free, 1" sandwich bread
- 30g (1oz) pecan pieces
- 3 large eggs
- ¼ cup (60ml) half-and-half
- ¼ cup (59ml) dark corn syrup
- 1 tsp. vanilla extract
- 2 tbsps. dark brown sugar
- 1/4 tsp. ground cinnamon
- 1/4 tsp. salt

Directions:
1. Place bread pieces in an ungreased 7" square cake barrel and spread pecan pieces evenly over the top.
2. In a medium bowl, whisk eggs. Stir in remaining ingredients.
3. Pour egg mixture over bread and pecans in cake barrel. Let sit 10 minutes.
4. Preheat air fryer at 325°F (165°C) for 3 minutes.
5. Place cake pan in the air fryer basket. Cook 15 minutes.
6. Transfer the pan to a cooling rack for 10 minutes. Once cooled slightly, slice and serve warm.

90. Apple Crumble Jars

Servings| 6   Time| 40 minutes
Nutritional Content (per serving):
Cal| 250   Fat| 8g   Protein| 3g   Carbs| 29g

Ingredients:

For Apple Filling:
- 455g (16oz) diced, peeled, seeded Granny Smith apples (approximately 3 large)
- tbsp. lemon juice
- 1 tbsp. gluten-free all-purpose flour
- 2 tbsps. light brown sugar
- 1/2 tsp. ground cinnamon
- 1 tbsp. butter, melted
- 1/8 tsp. salt
- 6 (4-ounce) glass jelly jars

For Crumble Topping:
- 2 tbsps. gluten-free all-purpose flour
- 35g (1oz) old-fashioned oats
- 40g (1oz) chopped pecans
- 4 tsp.s light brown sugar
- 1/4 tsp. ground cinnamon
- 1/8 tsp. ground nutmeg
- 2 tbsps. butter, melted
- 1/8 tsp. salt

Directions:

To make Apple Filling:
1. Toss diced apples with lemon juice in a medium bowl. Combine rest of the ingredients and toss to combine.
2. Ready air fryer at 350°F (180°C) for 3 minutes. Pour apple mixture evenly into jelly jars. Arrange three jars in air fryer basket.
3. Cook for seven minutes. Continue with the rest of the jars.

Making Crumble Topping:
4. Prepare the Crumble Topping while the apple mixture is cooking.
5. Once the crumble has cooked, add the topping. Continue baking for another five minutes.
6. Let jars cool 10 minutes before covering. Refrigerate until ready to serve, up to 4 days.

91. Amaretto Cheesecake

Servings| 6   Time| 35 minutes
Nutritional Content (per serving):
Cal| 280   Fat| 14g   Protein| 4g   Carbs| 29g

Ingredients:

For Crust:
- 85g (3oz) Corn Chex
- 95g (3oz) blanched slivered almonds
- 1 tbsp. light brown sugar
- 3 tbsps. butter, melted

For Cheesecake:
- 395g (14oz) cream cheese, room temperature
- 2 tbsps. sour cream
- 1 large egg
- 100g (4oz) granulated sugar
- ½ cup (118ml) Amaretto liqueur
- 1/2 tsp. lemon juice
- 1/8 tsp. salt

Directions:

To make Crust:
1. Pulse Corn Chex, almonds, and brown sugar in a food processor until it has a powdered consistency.
2. Put into a small bowl and add melted butter. Combine with a fork until butter is well distributed.
3. Press mixture into a 7" springform pan lightly greased with preferred cooking oil. Preheat air fryer at 400°F (205°C) for 3 minutes.

To make Cheesecake:
4. Combine cream cheese, sour cream, egg, sugar, Amaretto, lemon juice, and salt in a large bowl. Spoon over crust. Cover with aluminium foil.
5. Place springform pan in air fryer basket and cook 16 minutes. Remove aluminium foil and cook an additional 6 minutes.

6. Remove cheesecake from air fryer basket. Cheesecake will be a little jiggly in centre.
7. Cover and refrigerate at least 2 hours to allow it to set. Once set, release side pan, and serve.

92. Chocolate Soufflé for Two

Servings| 2   Time| 25 minutes
Nutritional Content (per serving):
Cal| 238   Fat| 6g   Protein| 1g   Carbs| 23g

Ingredients:
- 2 tbsp. almond flour
- 1/2 tsp. vanilla
- 3 tbsp. sweetener
- 2 separated eggs
- ¼ cup (60ml) melted coconut oil
- (3oz) semi-sweet chocolate, chopped

Directions:
1. Brush coconut oil and sweetener onto ramekins. Melt coconut oil and chocolate together.
2. Beat egg yolks well, adding vanilla and sweetener. Stir in flour and ensure there are no lumps. Preheat fryer to 330°F (165°C) degrees.
3. Whisk egg whites till they reach peak state and fold them into chocolate mixture.
4. Pour batter into ramekins and place into the fryer. Cook 14 minutes.
5. Serve with powdered sugar dusted on top.

93. Blueberry Lemon Muffins

Servings| 12   Time| 20 minutes
Nutritional Content (per serving):
Cal| 317   Fat| 11g   Protein| 3g   Carbs| 31g

Ingredients:
- 1 tsp. vanilla
- Juice and zest of 1 lemon
- 2 eggs
- 170g (6oz) blueberries
- 120g (4oz) cream
- ¼ cup (59ml) avocado oil
- 85g (3oz) monk fruit
- 240g (8oz) almond flour

Directions:
1. Mix monk fruit and flour. In another bowl, mix vanilla, egg, lemon juice, and cream. Add mixtures together and blend well.
2. Spoon batter into cupcake holders. Place in an air fryer. Bake 10 minutes at 320°F (160°F), checking at 6 minutes to ensure you don't overbake them.

94. Cinnamon Fried Bananas

Servings| 2   Time| 25 minutes
Nutritional Content (per serving):
Cal| 107   Fat| 1g   Protein| 1g   Carbs| 27g

Ingredients:
- 105g (4oz) panko breadcrumbs
- 3 tbsp. cinnamon
- 50g (2oz) almond flour
- 3 egg whites
- 8 ripe bananas
- 3 tbsp. vegan coconut oil

Directions:
1. Heat coconut oil and add breadcrumbs. Mix around 2-3 minutes until golden. Pour into a bowl.
2. Peel and cut bananas in half. Roll the half of each banana into flour, eggs, and crumb mixture. Place into the air fryer.
3. Cook 10 minutes at 280°F (140°C). A great addition to a healthy banana split!

95. Bacon and Maple Muffins

Servings| 12   Time| 30 minutes
Nutritional Content (per serving):
Cal| 110   Fat| 4g   Protein| 10g   Carbs| 13g

Ingredients:
- 250g (9oz) All-purpose flour
- 1 ½ cup (355ml) buttermilk
- ½ tsp. baking powder
- ½ tsp. baking soda
- 2 tbsp. butter
- 180g () finely sliced bacon
- 2 tbsp. maple syrup
- Muffin cups

Directions:
1. Combine the ingredients except milk to create a crumbly blend. Add this milk to the blend and make a batter and pour into the muffin cups.
2. Preheat the fryer to 300°F (150°C) and cook 15 minutes. Check whether they are done using a toothpick.

96. Air Fryer Brownies

Servings| 2   Time| 20 minutes
Nutritional Content (per serving):
Cal| 201   Fat| 10g   Protein| 8g   Carbs| 13g

Ingredients:
- 2 tbsp. of Baking Chips
- 30g (1oz) Almond Flour
- One Egg
- Half tsp. of Baking Powder
- 3 tbsp. of Powdered Sweetener
- 2 tbsp. of Cocoa Powder (Unsweetened)
- 2 tbsp. of chopped Pecans
- 4 tbsp. of melted Butter

Directions:
1. Let the air fryer preheat to 350°F (180°C).
2. In a large bowl, add cocoa powder, powdered sweetener, almond flour, and baking powder, give it a good mix.
3. Add melted butter and crack in the egg in the dry ingredients. Mix well until combined and smooth.
4. Fold in the chopped pecans and baking chips.
5. Take two ramekins to grease them well with softened butter. Add the melted batter.
6. Bake for ten minutes in the Air Fryer, making sure to place them as far from the heat source from the top.
7. Take the brownies out from the air fryer and let them cool for five minutes.

1. For making the glaze mix, the ingredients, and with the help of a brush, pour over the apple fritter when it comes out from the air fryer. Slice and serve after cooling for 5 minutes.

97. Coconut Pie

Servings| 6   Time| 50 minutes
Nutritional Content (per serving):
Cal| 236   Fat| 16g   Protein| 3g   Carbs| 16g

Ingredients:
- 50g (1.7oz) coconut flour
- 50g (1.8oz) erythritol sweetener
- 110g (3.9oz) shredded coconut, unsweetened, divided
- 60g (2oz) butter, unsalted
- 1 ½ tsp. vanilla extract, unsweetened
- eggs, pastured
- 1 ½ cups (355ml) milk, low-fat, unsweetened
- 30g (1oz) shredded coconut, toasted

Directions:
1. Set the air fryer at 350°F (180°C) and preheat for 5 minutes.
2. Meanwhile, place all the ingredients in a bowl and whisk until blended and smooth batter comes together.
3. Take a 6-inches pie pan, grease with oil, then pour in the prepared batter and smooth the top.
4. Open the fryer, place the pie pan in it, and cook for 45 minutes until pie has set and inserted a toothpick into the pie slide out clean.
5. Let pie cool until garnish with toasted coconut Then cut into slices and serve.

98. Cheesecake Bites

Servings| 4   Time| 45 minutes
Nutritional Content (per serving):
Cal| 198   Fat| 18g   Protein| 3g   Carbs| 6g

Ingredients:
- 50g (1.7oz) almond flour
- 100g (3.5oz) erythritol sweetener, divided
- 115g (4oz) cream cheese, reduced fat, softened
- ½ tsp. vanilla extract, unsweetened
- 2 tbsp. heavy cream, reduced fat, divided

Directions:
1. Place the softened cream cheese in a bowl, add heavy cream, vanilla, and ½ cup sweetener, and whisk using an electric mixer until smooth.
2. Scoop the mixture on a baking sheet lined with a parchment sheet, then place it in the freezer for 30 minutes until firm.
3. Place flour in a small bowl and stir in the remaining sweetener.
4. Turn on the air fryer, insert the fryer basket, grease it with olive oil. Then close it with its lid, set the fryer at 350°F (180°C), and preheat for 5 minutes.
5. In the meantime, cut the cheesecake mix into bite-size pieces and coat it with almond flour mixture.
6. Open the fryer, add cheesecake bites, and cook for 2 minutes. Serve straight away.

99. Tahini Oatmeal Chocolate Chunk Cookies

Servings| 8   Time| 15 minutes
Nutritional Content (per serving):
Cal| 185   Fat| 11g   Protein| 13g   Carbs| 18g

Ingredients:
- 60g (2.1 oz) tahini
- 30g (1oz) walnuts
- 1/4 cup (62.5ml) maple syrup
- 40g (1.3oz) Chocolate chunks
- 1/4 tsp sea salt
- 2 tbsps. almond flour
- 1 tsp. vanilla
- 95g (3.4oz) gluten-free oat flakes
- 1 tsp. cinnamon

Directions:
1. Let the air fryer Preheat to 350 °F (180°C).
2. In a big bowl, add cinnamon, the tahini, maple syrup, salt, and vanilla. Mix well.
3. Then add in the walnuts, oat flakes, and almond flour. Then fold the chocolate chunks.
4. Take a full tbsp. of mixture, separate into eight amounts.
5. Line the air fryer basket with parchment paper and place cookies in one single layer.
6. Let them cook for 5-6 minutes at 350°F (180°C).

100. Raspberry Cookies in Air Fryer

Servings| 10   Time| 25 minutes
Nutritional Content (per serving):
Cal| 110   Fat| 9g   Protein| 4g   Carbs| 8g

Ingredients:
- 1 tsp. baking powder
- 115g (8oz) almond flour
- 3 tbsp. of natural low-calorie sweetener
- 1 large egg
- 3½ tbsp. raspberry (reduced sugar) preserves
- 4 tbsp. softened cream cheese

Directions:
1. In a large bowl, add egg, flour, sweetener, baking powder, and cream cheese, mix well until a dough wet forms. Chill the dough in the fridge for 20 minutes.
2. Let the air fryer preheat to 400°F (205°C), add the parchment paper to the air fryer basket.
3. Make ten balls from the dough and put them in the prepared air fryer basket.
4. With your clean hands, make an indentation from your thumb in the centre of every cookie.
5. Add one tsp. of the raspberry preserve in the thumb hole. Bake in the air fryer for seven minutes.
6. Let the cookies cool completely in the parchment paper for almost 15 minutes.

101. Banana Muffins in Air Fryer

Servings| 8   Time| 15 minutes
Nutritional Content (per serving):
Cal| 211   Fat| 12g   Protein| 13g   Carbs| 18g

Ingredients:
Wet Mix:
- 3 tbsp. of milk
- 4 Cavendish size, ripe bananas
- 115g (4oz) sugar alternative
- 1 tsp. of vanilla essence
- 2 large eggs

Dry Mix:
- 1 tsp. baking powder
- 65g (2.3oz) whole wheat flour
- 1 tsp. of baking soda
- 1 tsp. of cinnamon
- 2 tbsp. of cocoa powder
- 1 tsp. of salt

Directions:
1. With the fork, in a bowl, mash up the bananas, add all the wet ingredients to it, and mix well.
2. Sift all the dry ingredients so they combine well. Add into the wet ingredients. Carefully fold both ingredients together.
3. Then add in the chopped walnuts, and slices of dried-up fruits. Let the air fryer preheat to 260°F (130°C).
4. Spray muffin cups with oil and add the batter into. Air fryer for at least half an hour.
5. Take out from the air fryer and let them cool down before serving.

Printed in Great Britain
by Amazon